Wild
PENNSYLVANIA

A Celebration of Our State's Natural Beauty

Text by Richard D. Whiteford

Photography by Michael P. Gadomski

Foreword by Governor Edward G. Rendell

Voyageur Press

First published in 2006 by Voyageur Press, an imprint of MBI Publishing Company, Galtier Plaza, Suite 200, 380 Jackson Street, St. Paul, MN 55101-3885 USA

MBI Publishing Company titles are also available at discounts in bulk quantity for industrial or sales-promotional use. For details write to Special Sales Manager at MBI Publishing Company, Galtier Plaza, Suite 200, 380 Jackson Street, St. Paul, MN 55101-3885 USA

Library of Congress Cataloging-in-Publication Data

Whiteford, Richard.
  Wild Pennsylvania : a celebration of our state's natural beauty / text by Richard Whiteford ; photography by Michael Gadomski ; foreword by Edward G. Rendell.
    p. cm.
  Includes bibliographical references.
  ISBN-13: 978-0-7603-2638-1
  ISBN-10: 0-7603-2638-X
1. Pennsylvania--Pictorial works. 2. Pennsylvania--Description and travel. 3. Natural history--Pennsylvania. 4. Natural history--Pennsylvania--Pictorial works. 5. Landscape--Pennsylvania--Pictorial works. 6. Natural areas--Pennsylvania--Pictorial works. 7. Wilderness areas--Pennsylvania--Pictorial works. I. Gadomski, Michael P. II. Title.
  F150.W47 2006
  974.80022'2--dc22

                          2006003130

Edited by Danielle J. Ibister
Designed by Jennifer Bergstrom
Printed in China

On the front cover
Bonsai-shaped red cedars endure the harsh conditions found on the shale barrens at Raystown Lake in Huntingdon County.

On page 1
Autumn's great show can be viewed in the Laurel Mountains from Baughman Rock in Ohiopyle State Park.

On page 2
Waves form a sandbar off a small island on the northern corner of Pymatuning Lake.

On page 3
A dead tree reflects off the calm waters of a beaver pond in northern Susquehanna County.

On page 4
Mount Minsi in Pennsylvania is seen across the Delaware Water Gap from Mount Tammany in New Jersey.

On page 5
The marsh on Big Pond in Presque Isle State Park takes on a frosty look during winter.

On pages 6-7
The four corners of Pennsylvania: Lake Erie in the northwest (page 6, top); vegetation circling a pond in the southwest (page 6, bottom); asters and goldenrods in a clearing in the northeast (page 7, top); and Tinicum Marsh within sight of Philadelphia's skyline, in the southeast (page 7, bottom).

DEDICATION

To my wife, Terri, for her patience and support. To Jeff and Sherry Snyder and Linda and Gerry Thorpe for their valuable creative advice, and last but not least to Josh Leventhal for hunting me down and offering me this wonderful opportunity.
—Richard D. Whiteford

To my parents who had the good sense to raise me in the country. To my daughters, Lara and Tara, who both constantly give me lots of bragging material. And to my wife, "Smitty," who somehow put up with me every day.
—Michael P. Gadomski

On page 8
The Tobyhanna Creek takes a picturesque slide over resistant sandstone at Warnertown Falls on the Pocono Plateau.

On page 9
The sun sets over Lake Erie.

On the title page
Mountain laurel grows on the thin, rocky soil of Indian Wells Overlook at Big Flat Laurel State Forest Natural Area in Rothrock State Forest.

Inset on the title page
Dingman's Creek plunges 130 feet at Dingman's Falls in the Delaware Water Gap National Recreation Area.

Left
The mirror-like waters of Promised Land Lake reflect autumn's tapestry on the Pocono Plateau.

ACKNOWLEDGMENTS

I would like to acknowledge Stephen J. Schweitzer and Robert T Haibach and the many other dedicated individuals of the Pennsylvania Game Commission; A. Gerald Zvirblis of Penn-Period Fossil Plants; Melody Farrin and the staff of the Western Pennsylvania Conservancy; Charlie Broadwater and my other former co-workers in the Pennsylvania Bureau of State Parks and the Bureau of Forestry; and Josh Leventhal and Danielle Ibister, my editors at Voyageur Press, for their direction, guidance and patience.
—Michael P. Gadomski

CONTENTS

By Governor
Edward G. Rendell

Above
A remnant old-growth forest is preserved at Heart's Content Scenic Area in the Allegheny National Forest.

Left
Delicate spring wildflowers cling to the edge of Hyner Mountain at Hyner View State Park in Clinton County.

When William Penn founded Pennsylvania in the late 1600s, forests stretched from border to border, covering nearly 90 percent of the state. By 1900, nearly all the forests were gone, a byproduct of our industrial legacy. Coal, oil, iron, steel, and railroads, which helped to fuel this nation, also helped to fuel the demise of our natural heritage.

Today, thanks to the work of great conservationists who had the vision to set aside areas for public enjoyment and protection, we once again are blessed with the beauty of our woodlands. Forests now account for nearly 60 percent of Pennsylvania's land cover. Our state forest and park systems are among the largest in the nation. Contained within them are more wild and natural areas than any other state east of the Mississippi.

These forests and parks offer enormous opportunities for wildlife watching, scenic drives, outdoor recreation, and environmental learning. Natural resources once used for industrial growth now support a twenty-first–century industry—outdoor tourism. With 4.5 million acres of public lands, visitors never run out of places to go. And the experiences are ones they will never forget.

As governor, I have explored the variety of Pennsylvania's terrain and experienced the beauty of its landscapes. I have traveled through the deep forests of some of our wildest areas. On a clear, chilly autumn evening in Elk County, I saw the darkest skies in the east and heard the bugling of wild elk. I have journeyed along Route 6, a world-renowned scenic drive, stopping at spectacular overlooks and witnessing the enjoyment of travelers.

Experiences like these are captured in *Wild Pennsylvania*, a voyage through Pennsylvania's past and future treasures. Richard Whiteford's passion for our most precious places is captured in his descriptions of our forests and fields, flora and fauna. As a longtime environmental activist and writer in Pennsylvania, his knowledge of and excitement about these wild places run as deep as the valleys that carve them. With his own passion for wilderness and keen photographic eye, Michael Gadomski's use of light and color allow you to feel the cool shade of the hemlocks, hear the music of rushing streams, and smell the aromas of a Pennsylvania autumn day.

While *Wild Pennsylvania* cannot replicate an actual visit to our great commonwealth, its photographs and descriptions will immerse you in the wild character that has been so wisely protected for generations to come.

Above

A pair of bald eagles rest on the ice at the confluence of the Lackawaxen and Delaware rivers. The Upper Delaware River watershed has become one of the most important wintering areas for bald eagles in eastern North America.

Facing page

At the base of Hooflander Mountain, in Snyder and Northumberland Counties, the Susquehanna flows over picturesque rapids at McKees Half Falls.

PENNSYLVANIA'S ENCHANTED WILDS

Above
A male wild turkey stands proudly with his long
beard in a spring meadow on the Pocono Plateau.

Left
Wildwood Lake near Harrisburg has what is
probably the only wild population of American
lotus in Pennsylvania.

Joe-pye weed grows on an island in the Susquehanna River.

Pennsylvania contains a diverse range of wild and scenic areas, from the flat coastal plain along the Delaware River to the alluring bluffs and sandy shores of Lake Erie. Within its boundaries lie the eastern rolling Piedmont hills, cloaked in hardwood forest, that abruptly drop into the fertile, expansive Great Valley. Like giant sentinels, the Appalachian Mountains rise west of the Great Valley in a series of long parallel rows. The Allegheny Mountains follow like a distinct set of waves. The northern part of the state consists of glacial plateaus etched with deep ravines that, from the air, look like frost patterns on a window. The north-central area, untouched by glaciers, contains the Deep Valleys section. Shimmering rivers and chortling streams nourish this lush green landscape and its abundant wildlife.

In 1681, King Charles II gave the young English statesman William Penn a province in America. The king combined the name Penn, in honor of William's late father, and *sylvania*, a Latin word meaning "woods." Penn's woods, hence Pennsylvania.

A sylvania it was. Dense old-growth forests covered the entire province, from the oak-rich deciduous woods in the south to the mixed deciduous/coniferous, maple-beech-hemlock forests in the north. According to historian James Truslow Adams, pioneer folklore claimed that a "squirrel might have leaped from bough to bough for a thousand miles and never seen a flicker of sunshine on the ground."

William Penn appointed his cousin William Markham as deputy governor of Pennsylvania and sent him to America first. In a letter to Penn, Markham described the province as "a fine country if it were not so overgrown with woods." In 1683, when Penn had finally seen it for himself, he wrote, "Whatever men may say our Wilderness flourishes as a Garden, and our desert springs like a Greene field."

Pennsylvania's geological story is as fascinating as its colonial history. Who would ever guess that around 500 million years ago Pennsylvania sat below the equator and its eastern border faced south? During this tumultuous geophysical time, violent earthquakes and volcanoes created Pennsylvania's Great Valley region. The ancient Acadian Mountains muscled into the sky east of Pennsylvania where the Atlantic Ocean lies today. Earthquakes and other geological upheavals spilled ocean water into western Pennsylvania, where it settled into the Appalachian basin and remained as the shallow Appalachian Sea for more than 200 million years.

Around 290 million years ago, the African and North American continents shifted and collided. Several massive jolts shoved North America's continental edge toward its middle, crumpling enormous areas of land into the Appalachian and Allegheny mountains.

Just when Pennsylvania should have been settling into a long geological respite, along came another landscape-altering event. About 1.6 million years ago, an ice sheet purported to be three miles thick in places capped the North American continent. This glacier gouged out the Great Lakes basin. It crept south into Pennsylvania, scraping off mountaintops and creating today's Pocono and Northeastern Glaciated Low Plateaus and the North-western Glaciated Plateaus. When the final glacier retreated around 17,000 years ago, it left depressions in the earth, creating the wetlands of the Pocono Mountains.

Several thousand years after glacial retreat, verdant forests developed throughout Pennsylvania. White and black oak species dominated the central and southern part of the state, mixed with hickory, American chestnut, and pine. The cooler Appalachian ridges and plateaus in northern Pennsylvania produced red maple, beech, sugar maple, black cherry, hemlock, and white pine. The varying combinations of temperature, elevation, and soil type found throughout Pennsylvania created complex and diverse ecosystems.

Ancient, exotic animals hunted or foraged in Penn's Woods. The American mastodon and Jefferson's mammoth lumbered through the forests with swaying trunks and pointed tusks. Giant wolves, ground sloths, huge short-nosed bears, saber-toothed cats, and musk oxen haunted the wilderness. The extinction of these creatures appears to have coincided with the arrival of another mammal—man.

When the Native Americans settled Pennsylvania, the wilderness abounded with eastern timber wolves, mountain lions, wolverines, bison, lynx, bobcats, moose, fishers, beavers, elk, and martins, to name a few. All but the bobcat, beaver, otter, and elk are gone. During the

An aspen and a red maple share
the autumn sky in the Scotia Barrens
in Centre County.

twentieth century, the Pennsylvania Game Commission's reintroduction program reestablished beaver, otter, fisher, and elk populations. Of course, many of the generalist species that Pennsylvania has today—suchas squirrel, black bear, fox, raccoon, deer, opossum, skunk, mouse, vole, mole, and rat—were plentiful then, too.

Many game birds, such as wild turkey, heath hen, ruffed grouse, and quail, inhabited the woodlands, where they scratched through leaf litter in search of food. Ducks and geese passed in great flocks during migration. Pennsylvania's forests provided vital breeding habitat for migrating Neotropical birds. In the 1800s, passenger pigeons were so plentiful that John James Audubon reported a flock that took three days to pass overhead. Today, an estimated 379 bird species spend some time in Pennsylvania nesting or foraging during their migratory routes.

A white pine sapling makes its way up through a red pine plantation in the Susquehannock State Forest in Potter County.

Pennsylvania's waters once abounded with fish. William Penn was so impressed with their numbers that in 1685 he wrote:

Shad are so plentiful that, Captain Smyth's Overseer at the Skulkil, drew 600 and odd at one draught; 300 is no wonder; 100 familiarly . . . herring swarm in such shoals that it is hardly credible; in little creeks, they almost shovel them up in their tubs.

Lake Erie thrived with lake sturgeon, lake whitefish, lake trout, northern pike, and paddlefish that also lived in the Allegheny and Clarion rivers. Largemouth bass and several catfish species flourished in deep lazy streams, and native brook trout inhabited cold, rocky streams.

Blueback herring, alewife, and Atlantic sturgeon thrived in the Delaware River. Pennsylvania's eastern rivers teemed with millions of migratory fish such as shad, herring, striped bass, alewife, blueback herring, and American eels. In the spring, after the ice jams thawed, shad made their annual migration up the Susquehanna, Delaware, and Schuylkill rivers and also up many smaller tributaries, such as the Brandywine Creek in Chester County.

In the spring, after surviving a sparse winter, Native Americans left their winter lodges to congregate on the banks of the Susquehanna, the Delaware, the Schuylkill, and the Brandywine, where they cast their nets into the water and celebrated spring's bounty. At annual shad festivals, they played lacrosse, told stories, traded tools, and feasted on game and shad.

When the first Europeans waded ashore, many Native American tribes already inhabited Pennsylvania. The Delaware tribe, also called Lenni Lenape or "real men," inhabited the Delaware and Hudson river valleys. An Algonquian-speaking people, the Lenapes were hunters and farmers, growing corn, squash, and tobacco. The Munsees, a division of the Delawares, lived north of the Lehigh River along the Delaware River.

The Susquehannocks, a powerful tribe of Iroquoian-speaking people, lived mostly along the Susquehanna River in central Pennsylvania. A division of the Susquehannocks, the Conestogas lived just south of Lancaster, and the Shawnees lived along the lower Susquehanna River with a separate tribe in the north near Easton.

An Iroquoian-speaking tribe, the Eries, lived in northwest Pennsylvania along Lake Erie's shore. Other tribes may have inhabited western Pennsylvania, but there are no records.

What must it have been like when the Lenni Lenapes, fishing the Delaware, first gazed upon a great wooden ship with wind-pregnant sails? What must it have been like for the Europeans to gaze upon the Lenapes, the Lenapes to gaze upon the Europeans? The European dress of frilly shirts, lapeled jackets, knickers, high stockings, buckled shoes, and a three-pointed hat must have been terribly peculiar to the Lenapes. Likewise, men in breechcloths and feather headdresses adorned with bone and shell necklaces and body paint must have been equally curious to the Europeans.

The first Europeans to glimpse Pennsylvania were German and Swiss, who established small Pennsylvania Dutch settlements in Bucks County in 1630. A year later, the Swedes began exploring and building settlements. Finally, William Penn arrived in 1682 on the ship *Welcome*.

The explorer Lewis Evans, writing in 1755, gives an idea of what Pennsylvania looked like in the first few centuries of colonization: "All of America, East of the Mississippi…, is every where covered with Woods, except some interval spots of no great extent, cleared by the European colonets." He also referred to the wilderness as "an ocean of woods."

William Penn saw first the coastal plain at Pennsylvania's eastern edge, along the banks of the Delaware River, extending from Markus Hook to Morrisville. Traveling farther west, he saw the densely forested Piedmont Plateau that climaxed in the Highlands, the easternmost ridge of the Appalachian Mountains.

If airplanes had existed in Penn's day, he could have flown above the forest canopy and seen the Great Valley lying like a great trough between the Highlands to its east and the long, tall Kittatinny Ridge to its west. The Kittatinny, at twilight and dawn, looks like a giant dull blue ocean wave that is about to break upon the Great Valley.

From the airplane, Penn would have seen the corrugated chain of forested mountains spreading westward beyond the Kittatinny: the Tuscarora, Blacklog, Tussey, Jacks, Nittany, Bald Eagle, and Shade mountains. This chain of mountains presented a formidable barrier that temporarily retarded the westward migration of colonial settlers.

Turning north, Penn would have seen the glacier-honed mountain plateaus of northern Pennsylvania, from the Delaware River to the Ohio border. Like a tattered window curtain, the eastern plateau boundary sags down to Northampton County and the western side drapes down to northern Beaver County, near the Ohio River. Between the parted curtains lies the rough mountainous terrain of the Deep Valleys section of north-central Pennsylvania.

Finally, west of the Appalachians, Penn would have seen the Tuscarora Mountain front towering like a tsunami wave followed by successive Allegheny ridges before the landscape mellows into the southwestern Pittsburgh Plateau region.

In the dead of winter, it is hard to believe that prehistoric Pennsylvania was a tropical paradise. Freezing temperatures show off winter's artistry with frozen cascades of waterfalls and evergreen forests draped in snow. Only the haunting hoot

The setting sun intensifies the autumn colors as it hits the eastern shoreline of Promised Land Lake on the Pocono Plateau.

of the great horned owl breaks the frigid crystalline night calm. White-tailed deer root their noses in deep snow, foraging for food. Startled by a stalking predator, the deer snap their heads to attention and snort frosty clouds of breath into the air.

Come late April or early May, depending upon the part of Pennsylvania, spring decorates meadows in a magnificent multicolored tapestry of wildflowers and forest floors with trout lilies, bloodroot, and lady's slippers. White viburnum, dogwood, and mountain laurel spray the understory with white, pink, and rose-colored blossoms.

The woods fill with the music of croaking wood frogs rejoicing to the hills about spring's arrival. Spring peepers join the symphony from vernal pools and wetlands. Neotropical birds infiltrate the forest and fill the orchestra with the wood thrush's flute-like song, the robin's chortle, the oriole's chatter, and the phoebe's *fee-b-lee*. In the wetlands, red-winged blackbirds call out *conq-uer-ee* from the tops of swaying cattails.

Summer settles into the dense green forests, lush fields, and teeming wetlands for which Pennsylvania is famous. Sweet honeysuckle permeates the humid air on lazy evenings as fireflies twinkle in the dusk. Mockingbirds run through their repertoire while robins compete for center stage. Bullfrogs croak the base line for a symphony of crickets. The long loud rattle of cicadas on a hot summer's afternoon and the shrill cadence of katydids on steamy summer nights add treble to the music.

Largemouth bass jump into the air, breaking the glassy surface of a lake to catch damselflies, while bats dart errati-

Toward evening, elk graze in the clearings on Winslow Hill in Elk County.

cally across the lake devouring hundreds of mosquitoes. Muskrats ramble through the tussocks in the swamp and slither silently into a creek, keeling their tails to-and-fro as they navigate toward their stream-bank home, while water snakes lie loosely coiled on rocks beside the water awaiting their next meal.

Autumn sneaks up behind summer, brushing a stroke of red on poison ivy, Virginia creeper, sumac, and spicebush berries, alerting migratory birds to bulk up and head south. Bright yellow goldenrod and golden spicebush covered with red berries finally expose autumn's intentions. Shortly thereafter, the forest explodes into a firework display of dazzling colors. Sugar maples burn brilliant red and tulip trees blaze yellow, but shagbark hickories upstage the cast with fourteen-karat gold-plated leaves. Autumn's final dull brown curtain drops to the ground as the seasons turn full circle and winter closes its frosty grip on a bleak, naked landscape.

Pennsylvania's wild areas offer myriad opportunities for outdoors recreation. Crystal blue lakes, babbling coldwater streams, and deep meandering rivers provide places to cast a line and reel in a prize fish. Rivers offer challenging whitewater kayak and canoe excursions through forested gorges or just a lazy drift downriver in an inner tube on a hot summer's day. Some lakes and large rivers provide opportunities for thrill seekers to enjoy motorboats.

The Pocono, Allegheny, and Appalachian mountains lure hunters to climb steep ridges in frigid air and stalk trophies in boulder-strewn forests. The mountains offer trails across ridge tops, through craggy ravines, across flowering glens, and along rocky streams shrouded by hemlock boughs. Folks who hike or ski these trails enjoy superb seasonal scenery, wildlife observation, and panoramic views of farmland and towns in the valleys below.

Wetlands densely cloaked in cattails, skunk cabbage, and sedges provide havens for shy waterfowl, amphibians, and reptiles. Sphagnum bogs and fens harbor an array of rare plants, such as the carnivorous sundew and pitcher plant.

Pennsylvania's wild areas teem with natural treasures. For many, this scenic solitude provides sanctuary from a hectic life and replenishes the soul. Ecologically, these wild areas represent rare and valuable ecosystems.

Pennsylvania's pageantry of forests, fields, rivers, mountains, and valleys; its diversity of wildlife, from the majestic elk to the elusive least weasel, must not be taken for granted. We should not allow shortsighted, short-lived economic gain that benefits a few squander the commonwealth's wild areas. These natural treasures lure visitors from around the world to Pennsylvania for hunting, biking, boating, camping, sightseeing, bird watching, and hiking. They also provide future generations with ecological benefits such as clean water, clean air, and diversity of wildlife. Because we are of the earth, we need nature for spiritual solace.

Henry David Thoreau said, "From the forest and wilderness come the tonics and barks which brace mankind." In his book *The Journey's End*, Wendell Berry said, "Going to the woods and the wild place has little to do with recreation, and much to do with creation. For the wilderness is the creation in its pure state, its processes unqualified by the doings of people. A man in the woods comes face to face with creation, of which he must begin to see himself a part—a much less imposing part than he thought." An ancient Indian proverb says, "Treat the Earth well: it was not given to you by your parents, it was loaned to you by your children. We do not inherit the Earth from our ancestors we borrow it from our children."

These testaments illustrate that our bodies and souls need nature, and to maintain our humanity, I think we must stay close to nature.

A close-up view reveals abstract patterns in the Mississippian shale on Hyner Mountain.

Chapter 1

PIEDMONT

Above
Hundreds of various-shaped potholes are
eroded into the diabase rock in the
Susquehanna River at Conewago Falls.

Left
The rare white variety of red trillium, *Trillium
erectum*, can be found by the thousands during
April at Shenk's Ferry Glen Wildflower Preserve
in Lancaster County.

In easternmost Pennsylvania, a sliver of sandy flatland extends along the Delaware River from south of Philadelphia upriver to Morrisville. Moving westward, the Atlantic coastal plain gives way to the wild regions of the Piedmont and the Highlands.

Two important wild areas remain on the coastal plain. The first is Tinicum Island, a small island 2.2 miles long and 200 yards wide. Tinicum Island hugs the Pennsylvania side of the Delaware River just south of Philadelphia. It is not a young island. In 1862, settlers recorded it as being 2.6 miles long. Over the centuries, steady currents and occasional floods have carved four-tenths of a mile off it. Small as it is, Tinicum Island serves as an important stopover for migratory birds.

Just north of the island is the John Heinz National Wildlife Refuge, known locally as Tinicum Marsh. This tidal freshwater sanctuary harbors birds, turtles, muskrats, snakes, and other creatures.

The tide reaches Neshaminy State Park in the Delaware Estuary.

Colonists estimated that over 5,700 acres of freshwater tidal marsh existed on the coastal plain between Philadelphia and Delaware. In 1643, settlers drained most of it for pastureland. Today, much of the marsh area hosts the Philadelphia International Airport, oil refineries, port of entry docks, shipyards, and other industries. Only about 1,200 acres of tidal marsh remain.

One of the earliest environmental travesties in colonial Pennsylvania was the putrefaction of Little Dock Creek. Flowing through the early settlement of Philadelphia, the creek emptied into a spacious cove in the Delaware River. Lenni Lenapes, who called the cove Coocaconoon, paddled their canoes into this cove to trade with settlers. Later, William Penn established a public landing at the site, next to a row of houses known as Bud's Long Row and the Blue Anchor Inn. Legend has it that notorious pirates such as Blackbeard and Captain Kidd hoisted tankards of rum and pints of ale at the Blue Anchor.

Soon, settlement expanded upstream. Colonists Anthony Morris and William Frampton built competing breweries along the banks of Dock Creek.

Vines climb trees in the summer coastal plain forest at Silver Lake Nature Center in Bucks County.

An American sycamore's roots desperately hold the creek bank as the tree leans over the historical Brandywine Creek.

The Bethsheba Bower and Bath drew creek water for baths and dumped the dirty bathwater back into the creek. Then two lumber mills and a tannery arrived. The tannery dumped tannic acid used in the tanning process and sludge from animal hides into the creek. Eventually, the pollution became so bad that people suspected yellow fever incubated in the filthy sludge. In later years, the city converted Little Dock Creek into a concrete sewer channel and paved Dock Street on top.

A short distance inland from the river, the coastal plain yields to the Piedmont province that stretches from the Delaware River to the Great Valley. The general characteristic of the Piedmont is its gently rolling hills interrupted by the flat Delaware Valley in Delaware and Chester counties and the wide, flat Amish farm country of Lancaster County. This was the most fertile farmland of the thirteen colonies. Its proximity to the Delaware River allowed settlers to export meat, dairy products, grain, and lumber throughout the colonies and to Europe. Farther north and west, the plateau rises higher and steeper, culminating in the Piedmont Highlands before abruptly dropping into the Great Valley.

The Pennsylvania Turnpike, from Bristol to Harrisburg, takes drivers through the heart of the Piedmont. West of the industrialized eastern Delaware Valley, the land transforms into rolling farm fields punctuated by barns and silos. It then rises into the forested boulder-strewn highlands, much of which make up state game lands. A fun drive is on Pennsylvania Highway 94 between York Springs and Mount Holly Springs. It is like riding a rollercoaster. Your car points skyward as you ascend a steep hill. A sudden thrill hits your stomach while cresting the hill and you barely have time to grip the seat before nose-diving down the other side. This road traverses a series of hills through bucolic farmland and orchards.

In pre-colonial times, verdant forests covered nearly the entire Piedmont. The exceptions were a few natural glens, swamps, and some areas Native Americans burned to plant corn or flush game. But across most of the Piedmont, streams cascaded down rocky, hemlock-shaded ravines to the rivers below. Lichen-speckled boulders and craggy outcrops decorated areas such as French Creek State Park and Unami Hills. This inhospitable terrain discouraged settlement, keeping these areas somewhat wild today.

In pre-settlement days, the Piedmont was rich with wildlife. To entice Europeans to move to Pennsylvania, William Penn described nature's bounty as it existed then:

The food, the woods yield, is your elks, deer, raccoons, beaver, rabbits, turkeys, pheasants, heath-birds, pigeons, and partridge innumerably. We need no setting dogs to ketch, they run by droves into the house in cold weather. Our rivers have

Spring brings out spicebush and skunk cabbage in the Great Marsh at the Edward Woolman Nature Preserve in Chester County.

also plenty of excellent fish and waterfoul as sturgeon, roe shad, herring, cadfish, or flatheads, sheeps heads, roach and perch; and trout in inland streams. Of foule, the swan, white, gray and black goose and brands, the best duck and teal I ever eate and the snipe and curloe with the snow bird are also excellent.

Water in the Piedmont drains into two main rivers: the Delaware in the east and the Susquehanna in the southwest. The Schuylkill cuts through the middle of the region, emptying into the Delaware River in Philadelphia; both feed the Delaware Bay. The Susquehanna River comes from the north, passing Harrisburg and flowing between Lancaster and York on its way to Chesapeake Bay.

Large creeks such as Brandywine, White Clay, Unami, Perkiomen, and Little Lehigh feed the Delaware River. The Conestoga, Octoraro, Pequea, Conewago, Swatara, and Muddy creeks feed the Susquehanna. These creeks twist through the Piedmont, offering beautiful scenes year round.

In pre-colonial times, spring brought great numbers of migrating sturgeon, shad, and American eel to the Susquehanna, Schuylkill, and Delaware rivers and Brandywine Creek in time to provide vital sustenance for hungry Native Americans that had toughed out a long winter in their lodges. Lenni Lenapes, Nanticokes, and other tribes packed up their belongings and traveled several miles to set up temporary camps for hunting, farming, and fishing at places along rivers where shad were easy to catch. The Native Americans dried fish; planted squash, beans, and corn; and hunted deer. It was a festive time of trading goods and tools, playing lacrosse, and giving praise to the spirits for providing this cornucopia.

European settlers pushed westward from Philadelphia through the fertile Delaware Valley, establishing farms along the way. The trail leading west from Philadelphia followed a Lenape path to where it ended on the eastern bank of Brandywine Creek in Milltown, now named Downingtown. A colonial-era log house still stands here today, and the trail later became old Route 30, or the Lincoln Highway.

A dense, foreboding forest stood on the west bank of Brandywine Creek. This land, recently purchased from the Native Americans, enticed settlers westward. They needed a road, however, to accommodate their wagons over the rough terrain and through the dense woods. In 1718, a Provincial Commission hired a French fur trapper named Peter Bezellion to build a road through the wilderness to the Susquehanna River.

Settlers cut vast tracts of forest across the Delaware Valley, making room for farmland. Gristmills, tanneries, iron mines, and lumber mills emerged, bolstering the economy at the new settlements that were eating away at the once ubiquitous forest. Millers built dams diverting water from streams into millraces to turn their giant paddlewheels. The dams prevented shad and eels from migrating upriver to spawn, drastically reducing their populations and depriving Native Americans, as well as riverine wildlife, of an important food source.

Above
Shadbush blooms on the Nockamixon Cliffs along the Delaware River in Bucks County.

Facing page
The Nockamixon Cliffs rise three hundred feet above the river at Delaware Canal State Park and harbor threatened and endangered plant species.

Rich veins of iron ran deep beneath the forested hills of the Piedmont. Iron furnaces, such as the restored Hopewell Furnace south of Birdsboro and Joanna Furnace north of Morgantown, belched charcoal smoke as they forged iron tools and products. It took immense quantities of wood to produce enough charcoal to feed the furnaces. Lumberjacks denuded entire hills of trees. Teams of horses dragged the logs to pits, where they were stacked in teepee-shaped piles and burnt to produce charcoal. Today, charcoal pits still pock forest floors throughout Pennsylvania. In short time, the Piedmont's once-lush hardwood forests became barren, stump-bristled wasteland. Rain eroded topsoil from the ravaged hillsides into the streams and rivers, killing fish and the aquatic life on which they fed.

As settlement spread across the Piedmont Plateau, colonists burned hundreds of acres of trees to clear land for pastures and fields. They also clear-cut tracts of

Both photos
The Nockamixon Cliffs are bathed in cool midday light and, later, warm late afternoon light.

timber for lumber to supply Philadelphia or export to Europe. As the demand for furs accelerated, tanneries increasingly relied on the tannic acid derived from hemlock bark. They located the factories in the hemlock forests and, in 1895, cut an estimated 800 million to 1.3 billion board feet of hemlock. In addition to cutting entire forests, tanneries dumped the used tannic acid into streams, causing serious pollution problems.

As if the human assault on the forest was not enough, disease and insects began taking their toll. In 1908, chestnut blight savaged the American chestnut, one of the most common trees in Pennsylvania. The chestnut played an important role in forest ecology. Its nut provided a vital food source for wild turkey, bear, deer, squirrels, and other animals. In 1925, white pine blister rust appeared, followed by the gypsy moth invasion of 1932. During the 1930s, Dutch elm disease took out thousands of American elm trees in Pennsylvania. It is estimated that, nationwide, more than 77 million elms died. In 1971, the oak leaf roller defoliated over a million acres of oak forest. Today, the woolly adelgid crawler's

Above
Pockets of wet meadow are found around the coastal plain forest at Silver Lake Nature Center.

Facing page
Flowers bloom in the wetlands at Silver Lake Nature Center in Bucks County.

Above
The rocks of the Bear Islands are
reflected in the Susquehanna River
at Holtwood.

Facing page, top
Dense vegetation lines the shore of
Lake Marburg at Codorus State Park in
York County.

Facing page, bottom
The unique serpentine barrens at Goat
Hill in Chester County, part of a state
forest natural area, contain rare en-
demic species of plants and insects.

larvae threaten to wipe out the remaining hemlocks, the Asian long-horned beetle threatens many hardwoods, and sudden oak death fungus threatens oak trees, but between the 1890s and the early 1900s, most of Pennsylvania's forested landscape looked like ground zero.

Alarm over forest destruction led to the founding of the Pennsylvania Forestry Association in 1886, and in 1895, Dr. Joseph Rothrock became its first commissioner. In 1898 and 1899, the Forestry Association set aside nearly forty thousand acres of what would become state forest. The tax sale lands included acres in Clinton, Clearfield, Lycoming, Monroe, and Pike counties. In 1906, Penn State University established the Department of Forestry to establish more state forests.

The westward migration of settlers necessitated transporting supplies from the east to the new settlements, and shipping lumber, grain, meat, and hides back to Philadelphia. Transportation needs demanded better roads than the existing crude cart paths. These paths crossed bumpy tree roots, rocks, and streams. They edged

The Pinnacle rises 530 feet above the Susquehanna River in Lancaster County.

Pinnacle Overlook provides a spectacular view of the Lower Susquehanna River.

Bear Islands rise from the Susquehanna River near Holtwood.

tenuously along steep rocky ridges and over cumbersome hills. Wagons constantly broke down from the punishing terrain or became stuck in mud or snow. In 1794, settlers inaugurated the first macadam highway, the Lancaster Turnpike, linking Philadelphia and Lancaster; by 1804, it ended in Pittsburgh.

The bustling economy demanded a better way to transport coal, lumber, whiskey, and grain to Pennsylvania's growing population, so the commonwealth built a 1,200-mile system of canals connecting Philadelphia, Pittsburgh, Maryland, and Lake Erie. Opening first was the Union Canal in 1825, connecting Reading at the Schuylkill River to the Susquehanna River in Middletown. The sixty-mile-long Delaware Canal, completed in 1832, connected Bristol to Easton where it joined the Lehigh Canal. In 1840, the Susquehanna & Tidewater Canal opened, connecting Columbia to Havre de Grace, Maryland, accessing Baltimore's ports.

Hindsight proved canals costly to build, constantly in need of repairs, and suffering much downtime because of floods and winter freezes. Even in good times, travel averaged only about thirty miles per day, and canal transportation quickly faded. This piece of Pennsylvania history is preserved at the Delaware Canal State Park.

Just as computers sent typewriters to the museum, railroads ushered canals to memory lane. In northeastern Pennsylvania, gravity railroads hauled coal from the Lackawanna Valley to Honesdale. The coal was loaded on railcars in the valley and pulled to the summit of Moosic Mountain by either stationary steam engines or actual horsepower. From there, the cars, relying on gravity, coasted down the other side of the mountain to the railhead in Honesdale. Here, the coal was loaded on barges and shipped by canal to Kingston, New York, then eventually down the Hudson to New York City. In 1829, the first steam locomotive in the United States, the Stourbridge Lion, made a test run in Honesdale. After several trials, steam locomotives eventually began hauling coal on tracks built beside the canals. A passenger rail service began in 1832, transporting people from Philadelphia to Norristown. Between 1836 and 1846, railroads sutured lines throughout Pennsylvania.

Thousands of years went into forming the beautiful potholes at Conewago Falls on the Susquehanna River.

Civilization's onward march ravished most wild places in the Piedmont, making it the hardest hit area in Pennsylvania. After Peter Bezellion slashed the first road west of Brandywine Creek, farms, mills, and villages followed. Today, Pennsylvania claims more road density than any other state in America. Every road attracts a replication of strip malls, culs de sac, and corporate centers. Street names like Cedar Glen Lane or housing developments named Oakland Ridge are hollow memorials to the wild that once was.

In 1681, William Penn declared in his Charter of Rights, "That in clearing the ground, care be taken to leave one acre of trees for every five acres cleared, especially to preserve oak and mulberries for silk and shipping." Obviously, his declaration went unheeded. The Piedmont Plateau includes only a few remnants of wild. The state park system set aside Nockamixon, Evansburg, Nolde Forest, Ridley, Blue Marsh, Codorus, and French Creek state parks and the Middle Creek Wildlife Management Area.

Although there are hundreds of potholes at Conewago Falls, no two can be found of the same design or shape.

Conservation organizations work feverishly against the developer's clock to protect biologically significant private lands such as the 2,400-acre Great Marsh and the Goat Hill Serpentine Barrens in Chester County, Durham Mine's bat hibernacula in Bucks County, watersheds such as Never Sink Mountain and Oley Hills near Reading, and Unami Hills in Montgomery County.

The biggest conservation effort in the Piedmont region now focuses on the 73,000-acre forest straddling southeastern Berks and northwestern Chester counties, known as the Hopewell Big Woods. It is the largest remaining forest in southeastern Pennsylvania. A large portion of the Philadelphia metropolitan area's water supply drains from the hills of the Hopewell Big Woods area.

Above
The Pennsylvania Game Commission's Middle Creek Wildlife Management Area in Lancaster and Lebanon counties serves as an important waterfowl migratory route.

Left
As many as 170,000 greater snow geese form a staging area during the spring migration at Middle Creek Wildlife Management Area.

Facing page
Over seventy-three species of wildflowers have been recorded at Shenk's Ferry Glen Wildflower Preserve.

Above
Redbuds grace York County's Gifford
Pinchot State Park in spring.

Right
Devil's Den in Gettysburg National
Military Park is composed of igneous
volcanic rock.

The Pennsylvania Greenways Program, sponsored by the Department of Conservation and Natural Resources, leads an effort to connect large wild areas by natural corridors, allowing creatures and people to travel from one contiguous wild area to another. Most natural corridors follow streams, which in turn help protect water quality.

Much of Pennsylvania's wild areas in the Piedmont Plateau are gone, but with efforts underway to restore and connect wild remnants, there is a good chance of reclaiming some of the Piedmont's natural heritage for the enjoyment of future generations.

An irregular shoreline borders Lake Marburg in Codorus State Park.

Chapter 2

RIDGE AND VALLEY

Above
Mountain laurel, the official state flower, grows abundantly
throughout the Ridge and Valley province as well as other
regions of the commonwealth.

Left
A rock outcropping just off the Appalachian Trail near
Lehigh Furnace Gap provides a splendid view down the
spine of the Kittatinny Mountain.

PENNSYLVANIA'S RIDGE AND VALLEY section is a rugged crumple of mountains that arch diagonally from the southwest to the northeastern corner of the state. On a topographic map, the ridges and valleys appear as if a giant bear swiped the central part of the state, gouging deep grooves into the terrain with its claws. Around 259 million years ago, the African continent collided with North America, causing the great geophysical upheavals that created these mountains.

Colonial settlers pushing west from the Piedmont region hit a dead end at the Kittatinny Ridge. The name Kittatinny comes from the Lenni Lenapes and means "endless mountain." This single ridge stretching 185 miles across Pennsylvania casts a bluish hue at certain times of the day. Local folks call it the Blue Mountain. Pioneers settled the fertile Great Valley east of the ridge, establishing farmsteads and hamlets such as Waynesboro, Chambersburg, Shippensburg, Carlisle, Harrisburg, Allentown, Bethlehem, and Easton.

Wild sunflowers blanket a summer meadow in Bald Eagle State Park.

Penns Creek flows through Bald Eagle State Forest in Centre County.

Hunters, explorers, and fur trappers were the rare few who traversed the Kittatinny, only to find what seemed like endless successive waves of mountains lying beyond. Second Mountain stood behind the Kittatinny, followed by the Tuscarora, then Shade, Jacks, Broad, Tussey, Nittany, Evitts, Dunning and Lock, Wills, Buffalo, and Brush, as goes the westward order of the Appalachian Mountains. Beyond the Appalachians, the chain of Alleghenies follows. This chain of mountains forced pioneers seeking westward destinations to follow the Great Valley south into Virginia and Kentucky.

Because the Ridge and Valley terrain was too inhospitable for human settlement, many of its wild areas remain today. The Appalachian Trail crosses from New Jersey into Pennsylvania near Stroudsburg at the Delaware Water Gap. It proceeds atop the Kittatinny Ridge southward all the way to the Swatara Creek just north of Indiantown Gap. From there, the trail bends north, crossing

Second Mountain to Peters Mountain, where it follows the Peters Ridge to the Susquehanna River. It crosses the bridge on U.S. Highway 322 at Duncannon and travels south. The trail crosses back over the Kittatinny Ridge, where it traverses farmland until reaching South Mountain. On South Mountain, the trail rambles through Michaux State Park. All told, the Appalachian Trail clocks 230 miles through Pennsylvania before crossing the Mason-Dixon Line into Maryland.

This stretch of the Appalachian Trail is notoriously strenuous. In his book *A Walk in the Woods: Rediscovering America on the Appalachian Trail*, Bill Bryson writes, "I never met a hiker with a good word to say about the trail in Pennsylvania. It is as someone told a *National Geographic* reporter in 1987, the place 'where boots go to die.' The state also has what are reputed to be the meanest rattlesnakes anywhere along the trail."

At the north end of the trail, the Delaware Water Gap offers a sudden and strikingly scenic threshold into Pennsylvania. This is true whether you are hiking or simply driving west on Interstate 80. The boulder-clad cliffs of the Kittatinny Ridge rise above the twists and bends of the Delaware River. The Lenni Lenapes called the gap Pohoqualine, meaning "river passing between two mountains." The river passes between humps of the Kittatinny called Mount Tammany, to the north, and Mount Minsi, to the south. In early July, colorful rhododendron blossoms splotch the steep slopes of Mount Minsi. In the parch of summer, rattlesnakes and copperheads hunt insects and rodents along the rocky ridge.

While Mike Gadomski stood squinting through the viewfinder trying to frame a photo of a water gap scene, he moved the tripod a few rocks over. As he lowered the tripod legs between some rocks, the buzz of a young rattlesnake instantly warned him that he was trespassing and would have to try that shot some other time.

South of the Delaware Water Gap, the top of the Kittatinny Ridge encompasses miles of state game lands. The

Balancing fifteen feet high, Sunset Rocks makes a striking feature in Cumberland County's Michaux State Forest.

ridge top is like the spine of a giant serpent whose tail ends somewhere in Kentucky and whose head rears somewhere in New York. Rough, rocky terrain underlies a mix of tall hickories, shady red maples, birches, and black gum. Five species of sturdy oak trees populate the Kittatinny, dropping acorns that provide a vital food source for deer, bear, squirrels, and wild turkey. Along the ridge top, vast rock outcrops afford spectacular views. To the east, the rolling patchwork farm fields of the Great Valley and the Piedmont fan out far below. To the west, the long narrow valleys

stretch for miles. Some of the best overlooks are at Weathering Knob, Bake Oven Knob, Bear Rocks, and Hawk Mountain.

There are only seven breaches in the 185-mile giant blue wall. From north to south, the Delaware River Gap is first. The Lehigh River cuts through the Kittatinny above Allentown; the Schuylkill River breaches it just north of Hamburg; Swatara Creek cuts through north of Jonestown, where Interstate 81 also swings through the gap. Next, Indiantown Gap and Manada Gap bookend a hump of the Kittatinny called Union Mountain. Much of Union Mountain serves as a military training ground for the National Coast Guard's Fort Indiantown Gap. The last breach is just north of Harrisburg, where the Susquehanna River gouged a huge gap through the great wall. It is hard to imagine the geological activity that occurred that carved these gaps through this prodigious mountain.

An oddly beautiful place north of the Lehigh River Gap, the barren slope of Blue Mountain was devastated by zinc furnace pollution blown downwind from

A rocky landscape forms Pennsylvania's "badlands" on Kittatinny Mountain along the Appalachian Trail northeast of Lehigh Gap.

Above
The delicate moccasin flower, or pink lady's slipper, blooms at Archbald Pothole State Park in Lackawanna County.

Facing page
Harsh weather conditions and frequent forest fires have created a low heath shrub land on the summit of Moosic Mountain.
This area harbors endangered species and is a priority area for The Nature Conservancy.

Palmerton over several decades. Not even hardy invasive plants that usually take over disturbed areas can grow in this toxic landscape. The area is an Environmental Protection Agency Superfund site. On the west side of Blue Mountain, a spectacular rock pinnacle called Devil's Pulpit overlooks the Lehigh River.

In late autumn, eagles, hawks, falcons, and vultures—sixteen species in all—dive, sore, and glide in circles above Hawk Mountain just northwest of Reading on the Kittatinny Ridge. The north winds of autumn, following the contour of the ridge, transport up to 20,000 raptors and about 150 other bird species on their migratory routes. For many decades, target shooters sat in the rock outcrops at Hawk Mountain and killed thousands of raptors just for sport. In 1934, conservationist Rosalie Edge purchased the ridge and stopped the slaughter. Today, Hawk Mountain Sanctuary is a leading biological research and educational center.

South of the Susquehanna River, the Kittatinny Ridge turns in a westerly direction. West of Carlisle, it takes a southerly plunge toward the Mason-Dixon Line into Maryland. Part of the Ridge and Valley province, but off on its own just south of Carlisle and east of Shippensburg, is South Mountain.

South Mountain hosts the Kings Gap Environmental Center and Penn State's Mont Alto School of Forestry campus. It also contains Pine Grove Furnace, Michaux State Forest, and Caledonia and Mont Alto state parks. The Meeting of the Pines Natural Area near Mont Alto represents a unique area in Pennsylvania where five species of native pine trees—white pine, pitch pine, Table Mountain pine, shortleaf pine, and Virginia pine—grow naturally.

On a cold, stiff March morning, I sat at a window in the Kings Gap Environmental Center high atop the western side of South Mountain. Across the snow-covered farm fields of the wide, flat Great Valley, the sun rose on the Kittatinny Ridge. The entire Kittatinny turned deep pink. As the sun continued rising, the mountain unveiled a host of other hues before turning a glistening silver from the full-day sun. High vertical mountains like those in the Teton Range in Wyoming claim fame for stunning sunrises, yet even if Pennsylvania lacks the vertical majesty of Western states, its horizontal landscapes take no back seat to nature's spectacular artistry. It was a remarkable sight packing just as much spiritual gratification as the Grand Teton. What the West has in height, Pennsylvania makes up for in breadth.

The cliffs at Mount Logan State Forest Natural Area in Clinton County are composed of hard, weather-resistant Tuscarora quartzite.

West of the Kittatinny Ridge, a great chasm zigzags down between the mountains on each side of the Susquehanna River, creating the Susquehanna Lowland Section. To the north lies the Anthracite Upland Section. Towns like Tamaqua, Pottsville, Schuylkill Haven, Jim Thorp, Hazelton, Wilkes-Barre, and Scranton nestle in small valleys throughout the mountains. Moosic Mountain in Lackawanna County provides scenic views for hikers and important habitat for endangered and threatened species. The building of a sewer line from Jefferson Township over the mountain to the Lackawanna Valley makes housing developments a serious threat that could forever ruin Moosic Mountain's wild haven.

On the west side of the Susquehanna River lowlands, the bulk of the Appalachian Mountains crumple Pennsylvania's heartland. The west branch of the Susquehanna River arches southwestward, defining the Appalachians'

Fallen autumn leaves rest on a lichen-covered rock in Bald Eagle State Forest in Centre County.

Facing page
Rock slabs litter a talus slope on Tussey Mountain in
Little Juniata State Forest Natural Area

Left
Copperas Rocks in Trough Creek State Park gets its color
from ferrous sulfate that precipitates from small underground
pockets of coal.

Below
Red cedars cling precariously to the shale barren cliffs at
Raystown Lake in Huntingdon County.

Morning mist floats over
Raystown Lake.

Green lichen covers the bark of an old-
growth eastern hemlock in the Alan
Seeger State Forest Natural Area.

northwestern boundary. The river's deep scar divides the Appalachians from the Alleghenies to the north and west.

North of State College, Bald Eagle State Forest contains some interesting and unusual features, such as the ancient pingo scars along Halfway Run Creek. Pingos are basin-shaped depressions in the forest floor containing seasonal stands of water. Seeps and springs etched these basins 15,000 years ago in the periglacial climate, or tundra zone, from the process of freezing and thawing. Pingos serve as prime breeding pools for frogs, toads, and salamanders.

Bald Eagle State Forest also contains the 152-acre Rosecrans Bog Natural Area, a high mountain bog thick with wild cranberry, mountain holly, northeastern bulrush, and highbush blueberry. It provides vital sanctuary for ducks, great blue herons, bears, and many amphibian species.

Rumor has it that one of the wildest areas in Pennsylvania is the White Mountain Wild Area in Bald Eagle State Forest. This 3,581-acre wilderness encompasses the east end of White Mountain. Sun-bleached sandstone rock outcrops adorn both the north and south slopes. These talus slopes create perfect habitat for the endangered Allegheny wood rat and the timber rattlesnake, and several caves and crevasses harbor many bat species, including the endangered Indiana bat. Little wonder there is scant sign of human activity in this area. Rocky overhangs, sheer cliffs, and rocky talus slabs lay like loosely strewn shingles on the steep mountainsides, making for unstable footing.

Bald Eagle State Forest contains remnants of virgin forests at the Joyce Kilmer Natural Area on Paddy Mountain. Virgin white pine and hemlock trees stand at Snyder-Middleswarth Natural Area. This area also contains 250 acres of old-growth hemlocks reaching 140 feet tall. Other old growth stands in the Ridge and Valley province include Detweiler Run and Alan Seeger Natural Areas in Rothrock State Forest in Huntingdon County. These forested areas cover ridges and pockets atop the molar-shaped convergence of Stone, Long, Thickhead, and Tussey mountains, southeast of State College. Another rare ecosystem is Bear Meadows, a large fen wetland cradled amongst the mountains.

The Juniata River chortles through the deep valley between Shade and Jacks mountains just southeast of Rothrock State Forest. The Lenni Lenapes called the Juniata River the river of shadows because the mountains shroud sunlight from its waters most of the time. The river flows from south to north, forging its way through the Tuscarora Mountains above Duncannon and joining the Susquehanna River at Clark's Ferry.

Jacks Mountain, above the Juniata, enjoys some chilling legends. In 1744, as tense relations between the settlers and the Lenni Lenapes climaxed, a fur

Left
Pin cherry blooms among the pitch pines in Franklin County's Buchanan State Forest.

Below
The forest canopy shows spring growth at Jakey Hollow State Forest Natural Area.

Above
The Devil's Potato Patch at Little Gap on Kittatinny Mountain resulted from intense periglacial weathering from a nearby cliff.

Left
This seed-fern fossil dates from the Pennsylvanian Period, some 248 to 290 million years ago.

Facing page
The sun sets over ice floes on the Delaware River just upstream from the Delaware Water Gap.

Facing page
Hemlock varnish shelf fungus grows on a fallen old-growth hemlock on state game lands in Fulton County.

Left
Yellow lady's slipper blooms at Canoe Creek State Park.

Below
The flower of the yellow poplar, or tulip tree, blooms at Sideling Hill Natural Area in Fulton County.

The Lackawanna Valley, viewed from Moosic Mountain, is rich with autumn colors.

trader named Jack Armstrong took a horse belonging to Musemeelin, a Lenape, in lieu of skins owed him. Armstrong and two other men rode off with the horse. Musemeelin, not understanding the white man's commerce, followed Armstrong with two other Lenapes to reclaim the horse. With trust severely lacking between both parties, Musemeelin killed Jack Armstrong and his men in the area now known as Jack's Pass. Armstrong's brother had Musemeelin hunted down and hanged for the murder.

In 1889, on Jacks Mountain high above Mapleton, a mysterious light appeared on the ridge. Some town folk climbed the ridge to the light and unearthed what looked like a decomposed body. Speculation labeled it either Jack Armstrong or another mysterious character named Captain Jack who, as the story goes, the Lenapes skinned alive. Captain Jack survived and became a fighter feared more by the Lenapes than any other white man. Lore has it that, around midnight, Captain Jack's ghost appears on the ridge and carries the lantern down to river's edge.

Rothrock State Forest, Trough Creek State Park, and Raystown Lake lie south of Huntingdon near the headwaters of the Raystown Branch of the Juniata River. The U.S. Army Corps of Engineers created the 8,300-acre, 30-mile-long Raystown Lake for flood control. Here, spring brings vibrant colors of wildflowers, mountain laurel, and rhododendron. Watch your step on the rock outcrops in the summer. Poisonous copperheads and rattlesnakes and the five-lined skink sun themselves along the edge. A large boulder balances precariously on the edge of a cliff above Great Trough Creek. Below the boulder, an unusual phenomenon called an ice mine, a hole in the earth that acts as a natural refrigerator during the summer, contains ice all summer long.

There are many parks and state game areas throughout the Ridge and Valley area—in fact, too many to cover in the space allowed here, so I hope no one is offended if I have omitted your favorite place.

The Ridge and Valley area of Pennsylvania is a wild and woolly area with a rich history and unparalleled biological diversity. With the pressures of a growing human population, the world's demand for natural resources, and the ski and casino industries, preserving this area for its wild heritage becomes more challenging by the day.

The rushing water of Wheelbarrow Run has carved a narrow channel through solid rock at The Tubs Natural Area.

Chapter 3

POCONOS

Above
Rhododendron maximum, native to Pennsylvania,
is in full bloom.

Left
The Tobyhanna Creek forms the beautiful
Warnertown Falls, which is now protected on
state game lands.

THE POCONO REGION is small relative to other geographic provinces in the state. It comprises roughly two thousand square miles of rugged glacial plateau bordered by Moosic Mountain to the west, the Delaware River to the east, the Kittatinny Ridge to the south, and it reaches northward to the town of Honesdale, in Wayne County.

Ancient glacial activity created a wonderland abundant with lakes, waterfalls, fens, and bogs, all nestled among mountains thick with mountain laurel and rhododendron, giving the Poconos the feel of Canadian backcountry. A popular destination for hunters and wildlife watchers, the region abounds with wild turkey, black bear, bobcat, fisher, river otter, beaver, and deer. Every season in the Poconos offers sensational scenery. The long, cold, snowy winters yield to splashes of pink and white blossoms of mountain laurel that herald the coming of spring. Lush, green summer mountains, cool sparkling rivers and lakes, and steep ravines dappled with colorful rhododendron blossoms help replenish the withered spirit.

Below
A pitch pine/scrub oak forest grows on the summit of Camelback Mountain at Big Pocono State Park.

A kaleidoscope of autumn foliage dazzles the senses with brilliant reds, yellows, and gold as the seasons come full circle.

Just an hour and a half drive from New York City and even less from the populous Interstate 95 beltway in New Jersey and Pennsylvania, the Poconos make a convenient and popular honeymoon and vacation getaway. Superhighways such as Route 80, 380, Interstate 84, Interstate 81, and the northeast extension of the Pennsylvania Turnpike make it possible to live in paradise and commute to work in the metropolitan areas. Today, this accessibility increases development pressure in the Poconos to three hundred times the rate of any other part of Pennsylvania, threatening to pave and develop the quiet mountain beauty, the very essence of its allure.

Three times over the past million years, glaciers advanced from Canada, covering the Poconos and sculpting their mountains with an icy chisel. The last glacier was over a mile thick. As the terminus of the glacier retreated, massive hunks

Above
Large cranberry is found growing wild in most of the Pocono bogs.

of ice broke off and remained. These colossal ice hunks, weighing several tons, compressed basin-shaped depressions into the earth. These kettles eventually became fens and bogs. As the glacier receded and ice blocks melted, silt and pebbles deposited by the meltwater created dams that blocked streams and created lakes.

Fen, bog—what's the difference, you may ask? The difference, according to nature writer John Eastman in his book *Swamp and Bog* is the acidity and nutrient level: "A bog is a wetland ecosystem characterized by high acidity and an accumulation of peat. A fen is a wetland ecosystem characterized by abundant nutrient inflow, low acidity, and the accumulation of peat—an alkaline bog."

While shooting photographs in the Poconos for this book, Mike Gadomski asked me if I ever went bog-wallowing. Having never before seen a bog, I met him at one named Jimmy Pond on a warm, sunny autumn day. Mike advised me to wear an old pair of sneakers and bring an extra change of shoes and pants. We hiked a logging trail through State Game Land forest for about two miles to reach the bog's edge. Typical of Pennsylvania, a new housing development encroached on one side of the bog.

A dense thicket of almost impenetrable highbush blueberry surrounded the eye, or interior, of the bog like a giant wreath. We found a place where water channeled a route from the eye through the blueberry to the wood's edge. The thick blueberry arched over the narrow channel, just high enough for us to crouch and wade under. The channel was deceptively deep, considering how narrow it was. We sunk to our hips in the cold water. Holding his camera and tripod above his head, Mike looked like a Navy Seal infiltrating enemy territory as he led the way into the bog's eye.

The eye comprised a large round flat area with humps of tussock sedge, clumps of autumn-colored blueberry, and leatherleaf bushes surrounded by large mats of

Right
A bullfrog waits for passing prey.

Facing page
Savantine Falls is hidden in the Delaware State Forest along Sawkill Creek.

golden-brown sphagnum moss, all interrupted by areas of open water. A beaver lodge stood at the edge of the open water near the center of the bog. Pitcher plant, with its purple-streaked leaves, grew in the sphagnum near tussocks. Another insect-trapping plant, sundew, spread its radiating reddish rosettes across the sphagnum beds like a series of spider webs. Tamarack and black spruce trees grew just inside the highbush blueberry boundary, providing a transitional level of growth around the perimeter of the eye.

The 16.5-acre, 12-foot-deep boulder field at Hickory Run State Park is the largest in the East and was designated a National Natural Landmark in 1967.

In the eye, Mike and I slurped along, trying to step from one tussock hump to another to avoid, as much as possible, damaging the fragile sphagnum ecosystem that contains many rare and endangered plants. Clumps of Labrador-tea and blueberry bushes pocked the landscape. Each step caused what looked like earth to jiggle like Jell-O. It felt like walking on a partially filled waterbed. When we stood still, bubbles gurgled up around the edge of the tussocks, releasing the foul smell of rotten eggs methane gas produced by the decaying sphagnum beneath the water.

Mike and his tripod slowly sank while snapping a series of shots, before he pulled his feet and tripod out of the muck to repeat the process again at a different spot. Bog-wallowing was fun, once, but I discovered I'm really a solid-ground type of guy.

The ecology in a bog begins when sphagnum moss grows near a tussock of vegetation and spreads. Sphagnum continually grows at the top of the mat and dies at the bottom. As new growth adds to the sphagnum mat, it weighs down the dead portion, sinking it deeper into the water. The dead portion releases tannins and acids that inhibit the decaying process, creating a static environment. Bogs are a good place to find preserved specimens of ancient pollens, seeds, and plants, which allow scientists to determine what kind of plants and climates prevailed during prehistoric times. In 1968, a dredging operation discovered a mastodon skeleton in a bog near Marshalls Creek. Radiocarbon tests date it to be 12,000 years old. It is now on display at the State Museum of Pennsylvania in Harrisburg.

Besides fens and bogs, the glacier also left behind a boulder-strewn landscape the size of six football fields in Hickory Run State Park. Widely fluctuating temperatures, caused by the advance and retreat of the glacier, fractured huge sandstone rocks into a clutter of thousands of boulders, some twenty-six feet in length. Today, the boulder field looks just as it did 17,000 years ago after the glacier retreated.

In other areas, the barren terrain left by the last glacier gradually transformed into sparse lichens, ferns, and mosses; through a stage of grasses and plants; to the lush forested mountain plateaus of today. A mix of hardwood and evergreen forests,

embellished with colorful florid mountain laurel and rhododendron and punctuated with huge boulders left behind by the retreating glacier, provide the hallmark beauty of the Poconos.

During World War II, this breathtaking paradise became a hideaway for GIs and their girlfriends. After the war, returning GIs married their sweethearts and honeymooned in the Poconos, making the mountain retreat the honeymoon capital of the world. Pink motels with heart-shaped beds and tacky hotels sporting ancient Greek facades clashed with the Pocono's natural splendor. Ski resorts popped up along lakes, and wide zigzagging ski slopes with mechanical lifts scarred mountainsides.

Many people, alarmed at the onslaught of development, realized the need to balance human activity with the need to protect the natural beauty and the

Long Pond, with its surrounding barrens, is one of The Nature Conservancy's "Last Great Places."

Above
A wild meadow shows autumn colors in southern Wayne County.

Facing page
The Lehigh River cuts a deep gorge at Lehigh Gorge State Park in Carbon County.

Clockwise from top left
Thick icicles hang from a rock ledge in the Lehigh Gorge.

Frost decorates cattails along Kleinhans Run.

Delicate frost crystals form a lacework pattern on
low-growing vegetation on the Pocono plateau.

Facing page
Morning autumn frost lingers along Kleinhans Run in
the Delaware State Forest.

The sun sets over Decker's Pond.

biological heritage of the Poconos for future generations. State agencies such as the Department of Conservation and Natural Resources' Bureau of Parks, the Bureau of Forestry, and the Pennsylvania Game Commission set aside blocks of natural land to preserve unique natural features.

Delaware State Forest contains Pine Lake Natural Area and Bruce Lake Natural area, where black bears roam and bald eagles nest. Hickory Run State Park hosts several mammal species of special concern, such as the northern water shrew, northern flying squirrel, fisher, snowshoe hare, and Allegheny woodrat, along with many rare plant species, such as Collin's sedge, bog sedge, creeping snowberry, golden club, and white-fringed orchid, to name a few. In Tobyhanna State Park and Goldsboro State Park, osprey nest and fish in the lakes and bobcat prowl swamps and forests hunting for snowshoe hare and other small animals. Many state game

Left
The prickly pear cactus bears beautiful yellow flowers.

Below
Native prickly pear cacti grow wild on the infertile shale ledges in Pike County.

Spring arrives at Spruce Swamp State Forest National Area.

Spruce Swamp is a boreal wetland in the Lackawanna State Forest.

lands border state park and state forests throughout the Poconos, allowing for some very large natural areas. This does not necessarily ensure protection for plants and animals, however, as each state agency sets different goals and management practices for their properties. For instance, the Pennsylvania Game Commission relies on timber sales as an important source of revenue. Some state forests sell timber and many in the western part of the state lease gas and oil permits. Other state forests allow all-terrain vehicles and many allow snowmobiles, both of which destroy natural ecosystems. An organization called the Pennsylvania Biodiversity Partnership works with these agencies to promote uniform conservation plans that best protect the state's biological diversity while allowing resource extraction.

The Nature Conservancy and other conservation organizations protect many areas that harbor endangered or threatened species or ecosystems. The protected Long Pond in Monroe County contains Rhodora heath barrens, one of the most significant moth and butterfly habitats in Pennsylvania. It also harbors pitch pine and scrub oak barrens, an important breeding area for Neotropical migratory birds. In all, The Nature Conservancy protects more than 24,000 acres of important habitat on the Pocono Plateau.

More than any place in Pennsylvania, the Poconos represent the current battlefront between nature and commercialism—between the survival of rare plants such as golden club, creeping snowberry, white-fringed orchid, and mammals such as the snowshoe hare, fisher, and the northern flying squirrel and the proliferation of roads, housing developments, shopping malls, and casinos. Time will tell if the Poconos maintain their wild natural allure or become the new metropolis bedroom community and gambling haven of northeastern Pennsylvania.

Cactus Bluff is a natural clearing in the Delaware Water Gap National Recreation Area.

White-egg bird's nest fungus grows on dead wood in Wayne County. Each "nest" is only about one-quarter inch across.

A nocturnal luna moth rests during the day.

Spring raindrops glisten on May apple in the Delaware Water Gap National Recreation Area.

Wild lupine and bracken fern grow in Pike County.

Above
Protected on state game lands from nearby encroachment, Jimmy Pond typifies a northern quaking bog.

Facing page
Little Bushkill Creek flows through the Stillwater State Forest Natural Area.

Chapter 4

Glacial Plateau and Deep Valleys

Above
Paper birch contrasts against autumn leaves in
Tioga State Forest.

Left
Morning mist rises over the Pine Creek
Valley in Tiadaghton State Forest.

THE NORTHERN GLACIAL plateau and the Deep Valleys region constitute a vast area extending from the northern portion of Wayne County in the east across the state along the New York border to the eastern half of Warren County, where it extends south to Route 80. The perimeter of the region travels east along Route 80 but dips down to include Black Moshannon State Park. Then it follows the west side of the west branch of the Susquehanna River to above Bald Eagle State Park, where it turns east just south of Worlds End, Ricketts Glen, and Frances Slocum state parks. From there, it slants northeast west of Wilkes-Barre and Scranton and comes full circle back to Wayne County.

Much of this region experienced two colossal geological events. The first occurred around 250 million years ago, when all of the continents congealed into the Pangea supercontinent. The African and North American lithosphere plates squeezed together, crumpling this region into plateaus. Then, starting about a million years ago, three glaciers scoured the plateaus east of the Deep Valleys

The roots of a yellow birch cling to the edge of a boulder at Beartown Rocks in Clear Creek State Forest.

section. Much of the melt from those glaciers flooded through the mountains to the southwest, carving out the valleys.

Forested mountain plateaus, breathtaking overlooks, deep gorges, cascading waterfalls, and shimmering lakes characterize much of this region. Ricketts Glen State Park, west of Wilkes-Barre, exemplifies this terrain. The 13,050-acre park contains twenty-two waterfalls, including the 94-foot Ganoga Falls caused by glacial melt erosion. Ricketts Glenn sits atop a plateau on the edge of the Allegheny Front, where at 2,449 feet on Red Rock Mountain, Grand View Point provides sensational views of the Ridge and Valley section to the south.

Northwest of Ricketts Glen State Park at Worlds End State Park, Loyalsock Creek cuts an S-shaped canyon through steep mountains. Above the canyon, a rock garden features huge boulders divided by narrow crevices, displaying the results of frost heave caused by the retreating glaciers. Fossils of ancient lungfish burrows, dating back 350 million years, appear in the red siltstone.

Route 6 enters Pennsylvania from New York at Matamoras at the Delaware River, climbs the Pocono escarpment, and crosses northern Pennsylvania all the way to the Ohio border at West Springfield. *National Geographic* magazine rated Route 6 as one of America's most scenic drives.

The enormous boulders of Beartown Rocks form a "Rock City."

It enters the northern plateau region from the Poconos at Clarks Summit and snakes along the east branch of the Susquehanna River through the Endless Mountains Heritage Area.

A few miles west of Mansfield, Route 6 crosses Pine Creek, entering an area designated by the state as Pennsylvania Wilds. On a map, the Wilds look like a giant green splotch in the north-central part of the state. The Wilds comprises 6.5 million acres, of which 5.2 million acres is forestland. It comprises 27 state parks; 8 state forests; 300,000 acres of state game lands; and 513,000 acres of the Allegheny National Forest.

On the northeastern edge of the Wilds where Route 6 crosses Pine Creek, a 45-mile-long gorge known as Pennsylvania's Grand Canyon zigzags through Tioga State Forest. Fifteen-hundred foot cliffs shadow Pine Creek in the gorge far below. The Pine Creek Rail Trail, a former Seneca path along the creek bank, connected the Iroquois living along the Genesee River in New York with the Susquehannock's Great Shamokin Path in the south, along the Susquehanna River. *USA Today* rated Pine Creek Rail Trail as one of ten great places to take a bike tour.

Legend has it that a group of settlers known as the Fair Play Settlers, some of whom were illegally squatting in Native American territory, held a meeting at a place called Tiadaghton Elm on the west bank of Pine Creek and declared

A small, high mountain bog graces Marion Brooks State Forest Natural Area.

independence from England on July 4, 1776. They had no knowledge of the Continental Congress making the same declaration at the same time two hundred miles away in Philadelphia. No written record survives, but the names Thomas, Francis, and John Clark, along with Alexander Donaldson, John Jackson, Adam Carson, Henry McCracken, Adam DeWitt, Robert Love, and Hugh Nichols, live on as accomplices in the event now known as the Pine Creek Declaration.

Another great legend from this region involves the famous Pennsylvania rifle regiment called the Bucktails, comprised of 315 mountain men from Forest, McKean, and Elk counties. In 1861, they met along the Sinnemahoning Creek at Driftwood and built rafts to float to Harrisburg, where they joined the Union Army to fight in the Civil War. On each raft, they erected a hickory flagstaff displaying the Union flag and a buck tail. Each of them also wore a buck tail on their hat. Legend says they were sharpshooters and greatly feared by the Confederate Army. They fought in many battles, including Manassas and Gettysburg. Just the sight of the buck tail on their hat caused many enemy soldiers to flee from the battlefield, or so the legend goes.

In the big green splotch of the Pennsylvania Wilds, state parks include, among others, Hyner Run and Hyner View, Kettle Creek, Ole Bull, Lyman Run, Patterson, and Bucktail State Park. It also includes 1.3 million acres of state forests such as Clear Creek, Cornplanter, Elk, Moshannon, Sproul, Susquehanna, Tiadaghton, and Tioga.

Within the Wilds exist 48,492 acres of designated natural areas. These natural areas contain important historic, geological, or ecological features. Many natural areas contain ecologically significant bogs, swamps, or old-growth forests that harbor rare native flora and fauna. For instance, Burns Run Wild Area and Fish Dam Wild Area, located in the southern portion of Sproul State Forest, provide important breeding grounds for the endangered Cerulean warbler, the elusive fisher, and elk.

Marion Brooks State Forest Natural Area contains an almost pure stand of paper birch.

Above
Turk's-cap lily grows along Pine Creek in Tioga State Forest.

Facing page
A leafless hawthorn stands in an autumn meadow at Ole Bull State Park.

The four seasons of the Pine Creek Gorge are on display from the Overlook Trail in Tioga State Forest.

Some of the pristine tributaries contain a naturally breeding population of brook trout. Caves throughout the region supply hibernacula for many bat species, including the federally endangered Indiana bat. Both areas are so rugged and remote that hiking is the only way to get there.

The Shawnee called them wapiti; we know them as elk. Before Europeans settled here, elk lived all over Pennsylvania. By the late 1800s, elk were eliminated from the state. In 1913, the Game Commission reintroduced some from Yellowstone National Park and South Dakota; today, around eight hundred elk inhabit the state. The elk range begins in Sproul State Forest and extends west to around Route 255. Route 120 runs diagonally through elk territory from Renovo to Emporia. Route 555 goes west from Route 120 at Driftwood through elk country to where it intersects with Route 255 at Weedville.

A few miles west of elk territory sits the 513,000-acre Allegheny National Forest. Being a national forest makes it susceptible to the influences of political pressure. The Department of Agriculture—which controls the U.S. Forest Service, which in turn manages the Allegheny National Forest—heavily emphasizes timber harvesting and gas and oil drilling over forest protection.

I traveled to the Allegheny National Forest to attend a public hearing to support protecting the Tionesta old-growth area. A 4,100-acre old-growth area, Tionesta represents the largest intact stand of old-growth forest found in the eastern United States between the Great Smoky and Adirondack mountains. Because areas like the Tionesta depend upon the whim of the political ideology of the sitting Secretary of the Department of Agriculture, a group called the Friends of Allegheny Wilderness is working to get the valuable area federally protected under the National Wilderness Act. This would limit logging, oil and gas drilling, and other non-conservation activities.

Kirk Johnson, the executive director of the Friends of Allegheny Wilderness, and Rachel Martin and Jim Kleissler of Allegheny Defense took me hiking in the Tionesta area before the hearing. It was like going back in time and seeing Pennsylvania before European settlement. Giant hemlock trees shrouded the earth in darkness, allowing only streaks of sunlight through their thick boughs to mingle in the morning mist. A thick blanket of moss and ferns covered old fallen trees, making them barely discernable. The melodic song of the wood thrush broke the silence, and the spicy fragrance of hemlocks, ferns, moss, and wildflowers filled the air.

Above
A waxing moon rises over a frosty winter meadow in Elk County.

Facing page
The rising sun breaks though the morning mist on Hyner Mountain in Sproul State Forest.

It was a thrill to see virgin undisturbed nature. I wondered what undiscovered plants, insects, and other microorganisms reside there. Tionesta is only one area within the Allegheny National Forest for which Friends of Allegheny Wilderness is seeking Wilderness Act protection. They have identified seven other ecologically important areas and, if successful, will set aside about 12 percent of the Allegheny National Forest as protected wilderness.

We understand very little about biological diversity. What comprises an undisturbed ecosystem? What interdependent relationships exist between a species and its ecosystems? We don't know, yet we are destroying ecosystems at an alarming rate. Cornell, Penn State, Yale School of Forestry, and Clarion University have several research projects going on in the Tionesta area to find answers. Clarion University researchers discovered a native population of gilt darters and mountain brook lampreys in the West Branch Millstone Creek, where the forest service plans to build logging roads and do extensive logging. Pennsylvania lists both fish as threatened species.

In the Tionesta area, tornado damage from a 1985 storm devastated several acres of old-growth forest. Seeing what nature can do on its own, and knowing about the forest service's proposed logging, gas, and oil plans, I clearly understood the importance of protecting these untrammeled remnants of wild places. After all, preserving 12 percent wilderness is not asking for that much.

South of the Allegheny National Forest, Bald Eagle State Park is a good place to see the contrast between the Ridge and Valley area and the northern plateau. To the east, Bald Eagle Mountain forms the last long western wall of the Ridge and Valley region. To the west, the glacial plateau comprises short, bunched-together mounds of mountains that, to me, look like giant loaves of bread. Traveling west on Route 80 between Milesburg and Snow Shoe, the highway curves around the base of where the Alleghenies' distinctive northern ridge fuses into the crumpled northern plateaus, providing another visual contrast between the two regions.

The Black Moshannon State Park covers 3,394 acres and encompasses a 250-acre lake in the Alleghenies northwest of State College. In 1737, the explorer Conrad Weiser said, "the wood is so thick, that for a mile at a time we could not find a place the size of a hand where the sunshine could penetrate, even in the clearest day." After extensive logging at the turn of the century, today's second-growth forests don't measure up to Weiser's description.

The northern plateau area is large and wild. Folks occasionally report cougar sightings, even though the predator supposedly no longer lives in the state. This vast region harbors ermine, the long-tailed weasel, fisher, black bear, mink, river otter, elk, snowshoe hare, and bobcat. It makes an important migratory bird breeding

A pure stand of gray birch grows in Wayne County.

and feeding area, and its swamps and bogs contain many rare plants. Some of the cleanest tributaries in the state, containing many rare fish species, wind through the plateau. Today, the endless forests and vistas make it hard to imagine this region's barrenness in the late 1800s after the timber industry almost completely denuded it of flora and fauna.

We must not forget the environmental damage done to this region from reckless deforestation, mining, and industrialization. It took over two hundred years and millions of dollars in forest restoration, stream cleanup, and ecosystem restoration—along with reintroducing elk, fisher, and otter—to restore the environment to a condition that pales to its original biological bounty. Today, we face deciding how to balance economic stimulation in this region with protecting the wild and natural areas that we worked so hard to restore. Will history repeat itself or will we learn from our mistakes?

Clockwise from top left
Wool grass thrives at Wallace Sphagnum Bog in Moshannon State Forest.

Ferns and skunk cabbage intermingle in the Susquehannock State Forest.

Naturalized foxgloves grow in Cook Forest State Park.

Like fingers, the roots of an old-growth white pine and eastern hemlock reach for soil in Cook Forest State Park.

Above
Winter comes to the old-growth forest of Heart's Content in the Allegheny National Forest.

Left
American sycamores stand in Sinnemahoning State Park.

Facing page
A frozen spring seeps off High Rocks along the Loyalsock Creek at Worlds End State Park.

Above
Water rushes around sandstone
boulders in Porcupine Hollow Run
in Elk County.

Left
A rainbow forms at a spring seep on
High Rocks at Worlds End State Park.

Facing page
Hick's Run flows through Elk
State Forest.

Above
The prairie-like fields, managed by the Pennsylvania Game Commission on the reclaimed strip mine at German Settlement, provide a vital habitat for the state's declining grassland bird species.

Facing page
Hyner Mountain, at Hyner View State Park, glows in the warm setting sun.

Chapter 5

GLACIAL NORTHWEST

Above
Wild morning glory blooms at Presque Isle State Park.

Left
The sun sets over a summer wildflower meadow at the
Erie National Wildlife Refuge.

THE GLACIAL NORTHWEST plateau region of Pennsylvania lies west of the Allegheny National Forest and extends to Lake Erie. Its boundary follows the Ohio border south to New Beaver, where it bends northeast through the middle of Venango County, near Oil City, and goes back to western Warren County, following the footprint of glaciers that once covered this region.

French Creek provides the region's dominate watershed. It begins near Sherman, New York, and covers 1,235 square miles down to Franklin, Pennsylvania. Conservationists and scientists recognize French Creek as the most ecologically significant waterway in Pennsylvania. The watershed is made up of many rare or unique natural communities. It is home to 158 of the state's rarest birds, plants, reptiles and insects including 89 fish species and 27 species of native freshwater mussels, including the federally designated endangered Clubshell and the Northern riffleshell mussels. Ancient glaciers carved five natural lakes in this region, including Lake Pleasant, Lake LeBoeuf, Edinboro Lake, Conneaut Lake, and Sugar Lake.

Presque Isle State Park consists of a 3,200-acre peninsula hooking eastward into Lake Erie. Despite being a recreational landmark hosting over four million visitors a year, it is also an ecological hot spot. Six distinct ecosystems function in the park, each providing habitat for a different variety of species. Over 320 bird species rely on the Presque Isle for feeding, breeding, and nesting. Over thirty-nine of these species' populations have dwindled enough to qualify as species of special concern.

Bordering the shores of Lake Erie is Pennsylvania's newest park, Erie Bluffs, a 540-acre tract of land shadowed by 90-foot bluffs. This park contains old-growth

A piece of driftwood is stranded in Pymatuning Lake.

A pair of vibrant, poisonous fly agaric mushrooms grow in Crawford County.

forest, unique oak savannah sand barrens, many endangered plants, and pristine wetlands. The Western Pennsylvania Conservancy identified this area as one of Erie County's most important biologically diverse areas. At the same time, the Sierra Club listed it in their "America's Great Outdoors" report as one of the most endangered wild areas in the country due to development pressures.

Lake Erie draws great numbers of migrating waterfowl from across northwestern Pennsylvania. Two wild areas dedicated to waterfowl conservation are Pymatuning State Park and the Erie National Wildlife Refuge. Pymatuning—an unusual name, you may think. Usually, unusual words originate from Native American language and Pennsylvania has plenty. Pymatuning comes from an Iroquoian word meaning "crooked-mouthed man's dwelling place." The story goes the Senecas named the area after a leader from an Erie tribe living in that area who was a notorious liar.

Above
Water lilies decorate a summer marsh in Crawford County.

Facing page
Blue flag iris bloom in Lowville Fern, a Western Pennsylvania Conservancy project.

Before the glaciers arrived, the area formed part of a large prehistoric lake. The glaciers advanced and retreated at least three times, pushing out vast amounts of water, creating Slippery Rock Gorge, and redirecting Muddy Creek and Slippery Rock Creek. During the final retreat, the glacier scoured and flattened the land, leaving a vast swamp that drained water into the Shenango and Ohio river valleys.

Due to flooding after heavy rains, the state built a dam in these valleys in 1913 for flood control and water conservation, creating the 17,000-acre Pymatuning Lake. The lake stretches sixteen miles long, with seventy miles of shoreline making it Pennsylvania's largest body of water within state boundaries. Today, Pymatuning is a famous waterfowl management and hunting area and has a waterfowl museum that displays more than three hundred mounted specimens.

Erie National Wildlife Refuge consists of two disparate land parcels. The Sugar Lake Division contains 5,206 acres of beaver pond, marshlands, and forested slopes.

Bracken fern grow under hemlocks and tamaracks in Wattsburg Fern.

Woodcock Creek flows to the north and Lake Creek flows to the south. The Seneca Division lies ten miles north of Sugar Lake and consists of 3,571 acres of wetlands and forests fed by Muddy Creek and Dead Creek. Several duck species rely on this vital habitat, including wood ducks, mallards, blue-winged teal, green-winged teal, black ducks, golden-eye, ring-necked ducks, American wigeon, hooded mergansers, bufflehead, scaup, and of course Canada geese. Raptors such as eagles, red-tailed hawks, ospreys, and American kestrels hunt throughout the forest and wetlands.

Many people don't know that northwestern Pennsylvania has oil deposits. Yet the world's oil industry began along Oil Creek, just south of Titusville, when Colonel Edwin Drake struck oil in 1859 after drilling down just sixty-nine feet. Today, the Pennsylvania Historical and Museum Commission preserves much of that history at Petroleum Central, the Drake Well Museum, and Oil Creek State Park. Petroleum Central, at its peak, was a bustling oil company town with no government, law enforcement, or public sanitation. It was reputed to be the "wickedest town east of the Mississippi." By 1875, the wells began to dry. Today, forested

Large rock ledges are found off the Rim Road in McConnells Mill State Park.

Above
As the evening mist rolls in, a bald eagle surveys Lake Creek at the Erie National Wildlife Refuge.

Facing page
Blazing star and goldenrod bloom in the rare relic eastern prairie at Jennings Environmental Education Center in Butler County.

hillsides, clean trout streams, beautiful waterfalls, and outstanding vistas replace the filth and din of the oil industry. Other parts of northwestern Pennsylvania still harbor many active oil and gas wells.

McConnells Mill State Park, covering 2,546 acres, surrounds Slippery Rock Gorge. An abundance of wild features—including rock outcrops protruding from the sheer walls of the gorge, giant boulders, waterfalls, and old-growth forests—won this area the designation of National Natural Landmark by the U.S. Department of the Interior in 1974. Legend says the name Slippery Rock came from the Native Americans for an exceptionally slippery rock where their trail crossed the creek. Folklore has it that oil from a natural seep oozed over this rock, causing the slipperiness and providing a great source of entertainment for the Native Americans. Michael Gadomski can attest to the viscosity of the rocks in this area after he, tripod, camera, and all took an unstoppable slide off one.

Three outstanding biking/hiking trails follow old railroad beds through Venango County: the Samuel Justus Trail, the Allegheny River Trail, and the Sandy Creek Trail. The Samuel Justus Trail rambles along the Allegheny River from Oil City south to Franklin, passing steep rock outcrops, old oil wells, and ridges covered with thick mountain laurel—all while providing great views of the river. At Franklin, the Allegheny River Trail continues south to Brandon. The trail passes Indian God Rock, a large sandstone rock at river's edge displaying petroglyphs dating from around 1200 A.D. It also takes travelers through two long, dark railroad tunnels. The Sandy Creek Trail branches east off the Allegheny River Trail at the Belmar Bridge, a 1,400-foot railroad trestle, and goes east to Route 322, where it links to the Clarion Highlands Trail.

George Washington crossed Sandy Creek in this area in 1753 on his way to Fort LeBoeuf, when the French occupied western Pennsylvania. Governor Dinwiddie of Virginia dispatched Major Washington to the fort to demand that the French withdraw from the territory. The fort commander, Captain Legardeur de Saint-Pierre, allowed Washington to return to Virginia without harm but warned that he would address any further trespassing with force. Eventually, France and England's squabble over ownership of western Pennsylvania led to the French and Indian War.

A 1,860-acre manmade lake dominates Maurice K. Goddard State Park. Bald eagles and ospreys nest along the shores and capture fish prey from Lake Wil-

Above
Wild sunflowers bloom along French Creek in
Crawford County.

Left
Staghorn sumac displays autumn colors at Erie Bluffs
State Park.

Facing page
A black oak savanna has overtaken an ancient lake sand
dune at Erie Bluffs State Park.

Ring-billed gulls line the Lake Erie shore at Presque Isle State Park.

The winter sun sets on the Lake Erie ice pack at Erie Bluffs State Park.

Above
Autumn leaves litter the sand dunes at Presque Isle State Park.

Facing page
Waves pound the rocky shore at Erie Bluffs State Park.

Above
Quakertown Falls tumbles fifty feet in Lawrence County near the Ohio border.

Facing page, top
At McConnells Mill State Park, eighteen-foot-high Killdoo Falls spills over an overhanging ledge.

Facing page, bottom
Slippery Rock Creek rushes through a 930-acre gorge at McConnells Mill State Park.

helm. The lake contains largemouth and smallmouth bass, muskellunge, northern pike, walleye, bluegill, crappie, catfish, perch, and sunfish.

Not only did receding glaciers leave bogs, lakes, and rocks, but changing climate conditions resulted in a long warm, dry period that created a prairie extending from the Midwest into western Pennsylvania. Prairie plants such as the beautiful rose-purple colored blazing star—which requires open areas, lots of sun, and dry soils—flourished in the new environment. At Jennings State Park near Slippery Rock, a thick clay prevented most tree species from reclaiming the twenty-acre remnant prairie area after the climate turned cooler and wetter. Along with providing sanctuary for rare prairie plants, Jennings is one of the few areas in the state inhabited by the endangered Massasauga rattlesnake. Twenty-five percent of Jennings State Park is prairie; the rest is woodlands and wetlands. Just south of Jennings State Park, Moraine State Park contains 3,225-acre Lake Arthur, which caters to boaters, anglers, hikers, campers, and bird watchers.

Geological events—such as the ancient ocean covering this area for eons, glaciers, and the vegetated wetlands—created valuable mineral resources such as soft coal, clay, oil, timber, and natural gas. These energy resources provided a boom for the industrial revolution, but the extraction process caused great environmental destruction. Today, many streams suffer from abandoned oil and coal-mine pollution. Companies strip-mined areas for coal and abandoned the areas without restoring them because paying the fines was cheaper than restoring the area to

Slippery Rock Gorge was designated a National Natural Landmark in 1974 by the U.S. Department of Interior.

its natural state. Ironically, one payoff for nature is that some of the abandoned long-wall mines now provide important bat hibernacula.

A variety of natural features grace the glacial northwest plateau region, including the bluffs along Lake Erie, Presque Isle, Slippery Rock Gorge, Pymatuning Lake, and the panoramic Allegheny River Trail. The biologically rich French Creek Watershed area comprises one of Pennsylvania's premier wild areas and its conservation effort deserves priority status to restore and preserve this pristine treasure.

Above
An apple tree blooms along the shore
of Lake Arthur at Moraine State Park.

Left
A small feeder stream flows into Elk
Creek at Erie Bluffs State Park.

Chapter 6

SOUTHWESTERN PLATEAUS

Above
The natural Meadow Run Waterslides flow
through Ohiopyle State Park.

Facing page
"The Flats" and Sugar Loaf Knob are framed by
foliage on the Laurel Highlands Trail in Ohiopyle
State Park.

THE SOUTHWESTERN REGION boundary begins at the Ohio border and the northern border of Beaver County. Traversing east across northern Beaver County, it bends northeast, running catty-corner through Butler County to just south of Route 80. From there, it runs east, south of, and parallel to Route 80 to the Allegheny Front near Port Matilda. Bending south, it follows the Allegheny Front to the Mason-Dixon Line, where it travels west along the West Virginia border, following the state line to where it bends ninety degrees to the north, back to where it began at the Ohio border and the Beaver County line.

As with much of western Pennsylvania, an ancient ocean covered this region for millions of years. Continental shifting created mountains that, over eons, eroded

and filled the ocean basin with debris, burying and compressing aquatic vegetation that eventually became the seams of coal that made the region famous. When the African continent collided with North America, it crumpled and raised the earth again, creating today's plateaus. Unlike the northwestern region, glaciers never covered this region.

The most prominent natural feature in this region, besides the plateau, is the wide confluence where the Allegheny, Monongahela, and Ohio rivers converge. The Allegheny River flows south from the Allegheny Plateau; the Monongahela River snakes north through steep forested ravines from West Virginia, converging with the Ohio River at a place the French and English explorers called the Forks

The Youghiogheny River curves around the hundred-acre Ferncliff Peninsula Natural Area in Ohiopyle State Park, which harbors rare plants.

From Mount Davis, the highest point in Pennsylvania, morning fog can be seen lifting in the distance.

Sulphur polypore fungus grows on Ferncliff Peninsula at Ohiopyle State Park.

With a passing storm in the distance, the setting sun draws long shadows from trees growing at the edge of a grassland at Friendship Hill National Historical Site.

of the Ohio. The word *Ohio* originated from an Iroquoian word meaning "great waters" and became the name of the wild and endlessly forested region west of the Alleghenies, commonly called the Ohio Country.

Imagine this area before humans arrived, when verdant forests of giant oak trees bore huge, expansive limbs and stretched endlessly overhead in a tangled canopy. Ancient hemlocks shrouded steep plateau ridges, allowing an occasional shaft of sunlight to illuminate the forest floor. Giant mottled sycamores lined riverbanks, shading the water and cooling it to a temperature suitable for native brook trout. Ferns, lichen, and moss carpeted the forest floor, blanketed fallen trees, and ornamented rocky outcrops. The only sounds were the wind, river, insects, birds, and perhaps the haunting howl of a wolf. Standing on an overlook, the first humans beheld the majestic confluence of the three silvery rivers converging in the dense forest; Native American sacred sites attest to the awesomeness of the experience.

As European settlers colonized the Piedmont and Great Valley, they pushed tribes west into the Ohio Country. Several refugee tribes—the Shawnees, Delawares, and Iroquoian-speaking tribes of the Onondagas, Oneidas, Cayugas, Senecas, and Mohawks—merged into a generic group called Mingos. For a time, the only white men to explore the Ohio Country were mountain men, fur traders, and explorers such as Conrad Weiser. Then the French built Fort Presque Isle on Lake Erie and Forts LeBoeuf, Venango, Ligonier, and Duquesne down through the Ohio Country in a quest to extend the French empire from Canada to Louisiana.

As land in the east became scarce, white settlers continuously violated treaty boundaries while moving west into the Ohio Country. England and France, already deeply engaged in the Seven Years War, struggled to claim this territory. The French, being strongly entrenched first, supplied the Algonquins and Hurons with guns,

Purple-stemmed aster and autumn-colored interrupted ferns mingle in Laurel Summit State Park.

Above
An old-growth forest survives in Hemlock Natural Area at Laurel Hill State Park.

Left
Northern pitcher plants have been introduced and are thriving at Spruce Flats Bog in Forbes State Forest.

Facing page
Fractured sandstone formations create an unusual landscape at Bilger's Rocks in Clearfield County.

ammunition, and whisky, instigating them to attack the English settlers and burn their villages.

In those days, river navigation offered the easiest means of travel, making the Forks of the Ohio a strategic military location. Whoever controlled the Forks of the Ohio controlled all three major transportation routes, so it was here that the French erected Fort Duquesne. The British eventually sacked the French fort, replacing it with Fort Pitt, which evolved into the city of Pittsburgh.

Endless forest covered the steep rugged plateaus of the Ohio Country. A series of Native American trails traversed Pennsylvania, providing the first established land travel system in the state. In the Ohio Country, trails such as Nemacolin's Path cut north to south and led to the Forks of the Ohio. The Kittanning Path ran from east to west leading to the village of Kittanning. During the French and Indian War, the military widened many Lenape paths to accommodate wagons and cannons; some of these routes eventually became today's roads.

After the French and Indian War, many of the tribes felt betrayed by both the British and the French. Chief Pontiac organized an uprising of local Native American nations against white settlers. A Delaware leader, Shingas, and a Shawnee leader, Captain Jacobs, rallied their tribes to drive the white settlers from the Ohio Country. Kittanning became the staging area for killing white settlers and burning their settlements. In September of 1756, Lieutenant Colonel John Armstrong led the Second Battalion of the Pennsylvania Regiment to Kittanning, defeating the uprising. In 1763, Colonel Bouquet fought a close but decisive battle against a band of Delaware, Shawnee, Huron, and Mingo warriors at Bushy Run. The following year, Bouquet met with Chief Pontiac and the Seven Iroquois Nations to discuss a truce.

As the Revolutionary War escalated, the colonial army had its hands full fighting for its independence from England. George Washington struggled to accumulate enough troops and money to fight the British along the East Coast. This left little protection for the settlers west of the mountains. In 1783, settlers in western Virginia and southwestern Pennsylvania, feeling disenfranchised from the populated eastern settlements, petitioned the Continental Congress to establish a new state—a fourteenth colony called Westsylvania. After the colonists won the war against England, little threat remained from the Native Americans, most of whom had already left the area, so Congress never responded to the petition and the effort died.

Waves of white settlers infiltrated the region, pushing Native Americans farther west into Ohio and Indiana. By 1800, Pittsburgh had swelled to some three thousand residents. Industries such as lumber, leather, glass, textiles, iron, flour, and whiskey flourished. During the War of 1812, Pittsburgh operated as an important shipping port for goods coming from the South up the Mississippi and Ohio rivers. From there, distribution spread by covered wagon to Philadelphia and other

Facing page
Spruce Flats Bog in Westmoreland County resulted from extensive past logging, which caused a rise in the water table.

Below
A rare plant in Pennsylvania, the delicate blue-eyed Mary blankets the forest floor on the state game lands at Enlow Fork Natural Area.

Above
Ferns and moss cover logs in Quebec Run State Forest Wild Area.

Above
The rock ledges at Jumonville Glen in Fayette County were the site of a skirmish between Lieutenant Colonel George Washington and French soldiers during the French and Indian War.

Left
Leaves gather in the interior of a small tectonic cave at Beam Rocks in Forbes State Forest.

Facing page
Adams Falls captures rays of sunlight in Linn Run State Park.

Both photos
Thirty-foot-high Cucumber Falls at
Ohiopyle State Park is seen in summer
and winter.

destinations, and in 1840, a canal system extended from Pittsburgh to Philadelphia. By 1850, over 25,000 people inhabited the colonial metropolis of Pittsburgh.

Settlers cut the dense ancient forest for lumber to make houses, bridges, wagons, and to export. Farmers cleared the flat plateau tops and the fertile valleys for pastures and fields. Large veins of bituminous coal underlying southwestern Pennsylvania, combined with the transportation hub at the Forks of the Ohio, greatly advantaged Pittsburgh during the Industrial Revolution.

The rapid onslaught of coal mining, steel production, and timber extraction devastated the region's environment as it made men such as Carnegie, Frick, Mellon, Heinz, Westinghouse, and Hunt rich and Pittsburgh the steel capital of Pennsylvania. The rivers ran black with pollution and sewage. Soot and smoke belched from smokestacks, darkening the skies and forcing many office workers to go home at lunchtime to change into a clean white shirt. Strip mines, sand and gravel companies, and timber companies carved up the land, leaving only fragmented patches of the once endless forest.

Eventually, many of Pittsburgh's smokestack industries left the United States and the Clean Water and Clean Air Act vastly improved the environment. However, a modern map exposes the latest threat to the remaining wild areas in the southwestern plateau region: Pittsburgh's sprawl.

In an effort to minimize the impact of suburban sprawl, the Western Pennsylvania Conservancy, working with federal, state, and local agencies, has protected over 85,000 acres, to date, of wild lands in this region. The Pennsylvania Game Commission has purchased thousands of acres of state game lands, mostly in small disparate pockets scattered throughout the region. Pennsylvania's Department of Conservation and Natural Resources has set aside many state parks and state forests that protect these wild and historic areas from residential development, though not from gas, oil, and timber exploitation.

The wildest area in the southwestern region remains the chain of the Alleghenies arching in a southwestward direction from Williamsport to the Mason-Dixon Line. The ridge top from Black Moshannon State Park south to Altoona comprises an unbroken chain of state game lands. Prince Gallitzin State Park sits northeast of Altoona, Gallitzin State Forest to the south. Yellow Creek State Park lies farther west of Altoona, just east of Indiana. South of Altoona

on the summit of Blue Knob Mountain, the second highest mountain in Pennsylvania, is home to Blue Knob State Park. South of there, between Route 30 and the Pennsylvania Turnpike, is Shawnee State Park. A few ridges to the west of the Allegheny Front, Laurel Ridge hosts a string of state parks: Laurel Mountain, Lynn Run, Laurel Summit, Kooser, Laurel Hill, Laurel Ridge, and Ohiopyle along with Roaring Run Natural Area and Forbes State Forest. In the latter, Mount Davis commands the highest elevation in Pennsylvania at 3,213 feet. The 70-mile Laurel Highlands Hiking Trail connects Johnstown to Ohiopyle State Park and also links to the 825-mile National Scenic Trail stretching from the Chesapeake Bay through West Virginia into Pennsylvania.

West of Laurel Ridge the last crest of the Allegheny Mountains, Chestnut Ridge, towers majestically over the Allegheny Plateau to its west. Pennsylvania Audubon designated the Laurel and Chestnut Ridge areas an important migratory bird flyway. This area provides critical habitat for endangered species such as the Indiana bat and the least shrew and threatened species such as the Allegheny woodrat, southern water shrew, and eastern small-footed myotis. River otters, bobcat, fisher, black bear, and timber rattlesnakes thrive here, too.

In the plateau region west of the mountains, state parks such as Ryerson Station, Hillman, Raccoon Creek, and Keystone maintain remnants of the wild plateaus. In addition, Fort Necessity National Battlefield, where George Washington lost the opening battle of the French and Indian War, lies between Uniontown and the West Virginia border.

Many individuals and organizations continue their ongoing efforts to protect the wild areas of the southwest region to preserve their ecological value, beauty, and quality of life for the benefit of future generations. Enjoy these photos, but be sure to visit these places so you can smell the sweetness of the air, experience the solitude, see the wild creatures, and feel the spirit of creation.

Left
Sheetweb weaver spider webs grace a late summer meadow at Prince Gallitzin State Park.

Facing page
Orb-weaver spider webs arch gracefully in the morning fog at Prince Gallitzin State Park.

Above
The sun sets on Raccoon Lake.

Facing page
Cumulus clouds drift over Raccoon Lake at Raccoon Creek State Park in Beaver County.

PENNSYLVANIA'S WILDS IN THE BALANCE

Above
Yellow lady's slipper grows at Canoe Creek
State Park.

Left
Wolf Rocks provide a lookout in Westmoreland
County's Forbes State Forest.

THE PRECEDING CHAPTERS take you on a tour of the physiographic regions of Pennsylvania. You read about what makes each region significant and viewed photos of Pennsylvania's splendid wild bounty in seasonal array. Yet, in spite of how much we cherish these panoramas, unplanned development and shortsighted human activity devour over 160,000 acres of this precious natural heritage each year. Moreover, the threat is far more serious than losing beautiful scenery.

Life developed on Earth in such a way that every species plays a vital role in maintaining the delicate web of ecosystems that carry on life's process. Prehistoric events such as glaciers, volcanoes, climate change, and possibly an asteroid destroyed certain ecosystems and certain species. However, human activity causes extinctions across all major groups of species in all ecosystems at a speed far exceeding any natural rate and prevents natural recovery with permanent obstructions.

Roads, sidewalks, driveways, rooftops, malls, and parking lots take vital habitat from the vegetation and wild creatures that maintain the web of life. Scientists estimate that one million species will go extinct in our lifetime. These structures also prevent water from filtering into the earth to fill aquifers and replenish area water supplies. Instead, impervious surfaces divert valuable water into storm drains, flushing it away. A healthy forest inhales carbon monoxide and exhales oxygen, controls flooding, and transpires moisture into the atmosphere. Human development subverts this natural process.

Conservation groups strive to stop the hemorrhage of Pennsylvania's natural areas and restore environmentally degraded areas. However, the age-old clash between unsustainable capitalism and conservation continues. Government, which showers hundreds of billions of dollars in tax subsidies on industry, rarely provides adequate funding for environmental protection and conservation on the premise that such measures will "hurt the economy." Yet if economists factored into the gross national product the costs for environmental cleanup and public health services, they would find protecting the environment up front cheaper than paying to clean it up later. Costly services, such as sewage and water treatment plants, now have to do the same work that wetlands once did free—before we drained them.

Previous generations passed environmental degradation down to us, but the buck has to stop with us. We can no longer afford to pass it further. By depleting Earth's biodiversity, we deny future generations the ability to survive with the same biological tools provided to us by creation.

We live in a new paradigm in which people must deem environmental protection a necessary cost of living, not a burden. We also have to understand that

Suburban sprawl in Chester County illustrates the residential threat to Pennsylvania's wild lands.

life is about more than what people want; it's about what the community of all living organisms need for posterity.

Perhaps an environmental epiphany struck someone in 1971 when the Pennsylvania General Assembly adopted article 1, section 27 to the Pennsylvania Constitution. It reads, "The People have a right to clean air, pure water, and to the preservation of the natural, scenic, historic and esthetic values of the environment. Pennsylvania's public natural resources are the common property of all the people, including generations to come. As trustee of these resources, the Commonwealth shall conserve and maintain them for the benefit of all the people."

That epiphany evaporated rather quickly. The commonwealth ideal failed to stand against greed and property rights. Between 1982 and 1997, industrial and residential development claimed 47 percent of Pennsylvania's natural areas while the population only grew by 2.5 percent. In 2000 in Chester County, the loss of natural land to commercial and residential development ran at a rate of two acres an hour. If this wasteful trend continues, most of Pennsylvania's natural treasures will be lost, leaving only a few remnants of yesteryear.

Many national organizations such as The Nature Conservancy, Audubon, The Wilderness Society, Trust for Public Land, and the Sierra Club work in concert with local land conservancies to raise money or change legislation for better land protection. State agencies such as the Department of Conservation and Natural Resources, the Fish and Boat Commission, and the Pennsylvania Game Commission are collaborating with a scientific advisory group called the Pennsylvania Biological Survey to create a unified statewide conservation plan to save the state's critical wild areas.

The sun sets on the Pennsylvania Game Commission's Conneaut Marsh in Crawford County.

The challenges seem daunting, but look at the formidable tasks previous generations faced and the remarkable accomplishments achieved from pioneer spirit, unflinching determination, spit, and elbow grease. Imagine the astounding challenge of building a railroad from coast to coast through rugged wilderness with no modern machinery; the same applies to building canals and electric power lines. Even more remarkable, in modern times, we put men on the moon.

If we apply that same will and determination to conservation, we can clean Pennsylvania's streams and rivers, protect its flora and fauna, and restore connective greenways to large protected blocks of wild areas. Once again, a squirrel might leap from one bough to another across the state and never see "a flicker of sunshine on the ground."

Conservation Resources and Nature Organizations

Audubon Pennsylvania
Olewine Nature Center
100 Wildwood Way
Harrisburg, PA 17110
Phone: (717) 213-6880
Fax: (717) 213-6883
http://pa.audubon.org

Berks County Conservancy
25 North 11th Street
Reading, PA 19601
Phone: (610) 372-4992
Fax: (610) 372-2917
www.berks-conservancy.org

Brandywine Conservancy
U.S Route 1
P.O. Box 141
Chadds Ford, PA 19317
Phone: (610) 388-2700
Fax: (610) 388-1575
www.brandywineconservancy.org

Brandywine Valley Association/Red Clay
Valley Association
1760 Unionville-Wawaset Road
West Chester, PA 19382
Phone: (610) 793-1090
Fax: (610) 793-2813
www.bva-rcva.org

Chesapeake Bay Foundation
Pennsylvania State Office
614 North Front Street, Suite G
Harrisburg, PA 17101
Phone: (717) 234-5550
Fax: (717) 234-9632
www.savethebay.org

ClearWater Conservancy
2555 North Atherton Street
State College, PA 16803
Phone: (814) 237-0400
Fax: (814) 237-4909
www.clearwaterconservancy.org

The Conservation Fund
Pennsylvania Office
105 North Front Street, Suite 400
Harrisburg, PA 17101
Phone: (717) 230-8166
Fax: (717) 230-8167
www.conservationfund.org

Green Valleys Association
1368 Prizer Road
Pottstown, PA 19465
Phone: (610) 469-4900
Fax: (610) 469-4990
www.greenvalleys.org

Heritage Conservancy
85 Old Dublin Pike
Doylestown, PA 18901
Phone: (215) 345-7020
Fax: (215) 345-4328
www.heritageconservancy.org

Land Conservancy of Adams County
670 Old Harrisburg Road
P.O. Box 4584
Gettysburg, PA 17325
Phone: (717) 334-2828
Fax: (717) 337-0730
www.lcacnet.org

Montgomery County Lands Trust
P.O. Box 300
Lederach, PA 19450
Phone: (215) 513-0100
Fax: (215) 513-0150
www.mclt.org

Natural Lands Trust
1031 Palmers Mill Road
Media, PA 19063
Phone: (610) 353-5587
Fax: (610) 353-0517
www.natlands.org

The Nature Conservancy
15 East Ridge Pike, Suite 500
Conshohocken, PA 19428
Phone: (610) 834-1373
Fax: (610) 834-6533
www.nature.org

Northcentral Pennsylvania Conservancy
P.O. Box 2083
Williamsport, PA 17703
Phone: (570) 323-6222
Fax: (570) 321-1697
www.npcweb.org

Pocono Heritage Land Trust
P.O. Box 553
Pocono Pines, PA 18350
Phone: (570) 643-2890
Fax: (570) 643-7922

Tinicum Conservancy
P.O. Box 206
Erwinna, PA 18920
Phone: (610) 847-8650

Western Pennsylvania Conservancy
209 Fourth Avenue
Pittsburgh, PA 15222
Phone: (412) 288-2777
Fax: (412) 281-1792
www.paconserve.org

Westsylvania Heritage Corporation
P.O. Box 565
105 Zee Plaza
Hollidaysburg, PA 16648
Phone: (800) 898-3636
Fax: (814) 696-9569
www.westsylvania.org

BIBLIOGRAPHY

Aron, Jean. *The Short Hiker: Small Green Circles*. Boalsburg, PA: Aron Publications, 1999.

Barnes, John H., and W. D. Sevon. *The Geological Story of Pennsylvania*. Harrisburg, PA: Pennsylvania Geological Survey, 2002.

Bonta, Marcia. *Outbound Journeys in Pennsylvania: A Guide to Natural Places for Individuals and Group Outings*. University Park, PA: The Pennsylvania State University Press, 1990.

———. *More Outbound Journeys in Pennsylvania: A Guide to Natural Places for Individuals and Group Outings*. University Park, PA: The Pennsylvania State University Press, 1995.

Cooper, Edwin L. *Fishes of Pennsylvania and the Northeastern United States*. University Park, PA: Penn State, 1983.

Czarnecki, Greg, and Karen Czarnecki. *Highroad Guide to the Pennsylvania Mountains*. Atlanta: Longstreet Press, 1999.

Dixon, David. *Bushy Run Battlefield*. Pennsylvania Trail of History Guide. Mechanicsburg, PA: Stackpole Books 2003.

Dwyer, Tom. *A Guide to the Allegheny National Forest*. Syracuse, NY: Trailside Publishing, 1999.

Eastman, John. *Swamp and Bog*. Mechanicsburg, PA: Stackpole Books, 1995.

Fergus, Charles. *Natural Pennsylvania: Exploring the State Forest Natural Areas*. Mechanicsburg, PA: Stackpole Books, 2002.

Fike, Jean. Terrestrial & Palustrine. *Plant Communities of Pennsylvania*. Harrisburg, PA: Pennsylvania Natural Diversity Inventory, 1999.

Geyer, Alan R., and William H. Bolles. *Outstanding Scenic Geological Features of Pennsylvania*. Harrisburg, PA: Pennsylvania Geological Survey, 1987.

Grimm, William C. *Birds of the Pymatuning Region*. Harrisburg, PA: The Pennsylvania Game Commission, 1952.

Guilday, J. E. *The Physiographic Provinces of Pennsylvania*. Carnegie Museum of Natural History Special Publication No. 11, 1985.

Haywood, Mary Joy, and Phyllis Monk Testal. *Wildflowers of Pennsylvania*. Pittsburgh: Botanical Society of Western Pennsylvania, 2001.

Illick, Joseph S. *Pennsylvania Trees*. Harrisburg, PA: Pennsylvania Department of Forestry, 1919.

Jameson, Franklin. *Narratives of Early Pennsylvania, West New Jersey and Delaware 1630–1707*. New York: Scribner's, 1912.

Kelly, Joseph J. *Pennsylvania: The Colonial Years*. New York: Doubleday, 1980.

Kershner, Bruce, and Robert T. Leverett. *The Sierra Club Guide to the Ancient Forests of the Northeast*. San Francisco: Sierra Club Books, 2004.

Korber, Kathy, and Hal Korber. *Pennsylvania Wildlife: A Viewer's Guide*. Lemoyne, PA: Northwoods Publications, 1994.

Letcher, Gary. *Waterfalls of the Mid-Atlantic States*. Woodstock, VT: The Countryman Press, 2004.

Macdougall, J. D. *A Short Story of Planet Earth: Mountains, Mammals, Fire, and Ice*. New York: John Wiley & Sons, 1996.

McIlnay, Dennis. *Juniata River of Sorrow*. Hollidaysburg, PA: Seven Oaks Press, 2002.

Merrell, James H. *Into the American Woods: Negotiating on the Pennsylvania Frontier*. New York: W.W. Norton & Company, 1999.

Michaels, Art. *Pennsylvania Overlooks: A Guide for Sightseers and Outdoor People*. University Park, PA: The Pennsylvania State University Press, 2003.

Miller, Randall, and William Pencak. *Pennsylvania: A History of the Commonwealth*. University Park, PA: The Pennsylvania State University Press, 2002.

Mitchell, Jeff. *Backpacking Pennsylvania: 37 Great Hikes*. Mechanicsburg, PA: Stackpole Books, 2005.

———. *Hiking the Endless Mountains: Exploring the Wilderness of Northeastern Pennsylvania*. Mechanicsburg, PA: Stackpole Books, 2003.

Mowery, Marci J., and Audubon Pennsylvania. *Susquehanna River Birding and Wildlife Trail*. Harrisburg, PA: Department of Conservation and Natural Resources, 2004.

Mulkearn, Lois. "Of the Face of the Country." In *A Topographical Description of the Dominions of the United States of America: A Topographical Description of Such Parts of North America as Are Contained in the (Annexed) Map of the Middle British Colonies in North America*, edited by Lois Mulkearn. Pittsburgh: University of Pittsburgh Press, 1949.

Newman, Boyd, and Linda Boyd. *Great Hikes in the Poconos and Northeast Pennsylvania*. Mechanicsburg, PA: Stackpole Books, 2000.

Oplinger, Carl S., and Robert Halma. *The Poconos: An Illustrated Natural History Guide*. New Brunswick, NJ: Rutgers University Press, 1988.

Ostertag, Rhonda, and George Ostertag. *Hiking Pennsylvania*. Helena, MT: Falcon Publishing, 1998.

———. *Scenic Driving Pennsylvania*. Helena, MT: Falcon Publishing, 1999.

Ostrander, Stephen J. *Great Natural Areas in Eastern Pennsylvania*. Mechanicsburg, PA: Stackpole Books, 1996.

———. *Great Natural Areas in Western Pennsylvania*. Mechanicsburg, PA: Stackpole Books, 2002.

Root, Douglas. *Compass American Guides: Pennsylvania*. New York: Fodor's Travel Publications, 2003.

Scherer, Glen, and Don Hopey. *Exploring the Appalachian Trail: Hikes in the Mid-Atlantic States*. Mechanicsburg, PA: Stackpole Books, 1998.

Shank, William. *Indian Trails to Super Highways*. Annapolis, MD: American Canal & Transportation Center, 1967.

Stutz, Bruce. *Natural Lives, Modern Times: People and Places of the Delaware River*. New York: Crown Publishing, 1992.

Thwaites, Tom. *Fifty Hikes in Central Pennsylvania*. Woodstock, VT: Backcountry Books, 2001.

———. *Fifty Hikes in Eastern Pennsylvania*. Woodstock, VT: Backcountry Books, 2003.

———. *Fifty Hikes in Western Pennsylvania*. Woodstock, VT: Backcountry Books, 1990.

Walter, Eugene. *The Smithsonian Guides to Natural America: The Mid-Atlantic States*. Washington, DC: Smithsonian Books, 1996.

Walton, Richard K., and Robert W. Lawson. *A Guide to Bird-Song Identification*, Peterson Field Guides. New York: Houghton Mifflin, 1989.

Weidensaul, Scott. *Mountains of the Heart: A Natural History of the Appalachians*. Golden, CO: Fulcrum Publishing, 1994.

Whitney, Gordon G. *From Coastal Wilderness to Fruited Plain*. New York: Cambridge Press, 1994.

Wiemann, Barbara L. *Pennsylvania Hiking Trails*. Cogan Station, PA: Keystone Trails Association, 1998.

Wilshusen, Peter J. *Geology of the Appalachian Trail in Pennsylvania*. Harrisburg, PA: Pennsylvania Geological Survey, 1983.

Young, John. *Hike America Pennsylvania: An Atlas of Pennsylvania's Greatest Hiking Adventures*. Guilford, CT: The Globe Pequot Press, 2001.

INDEX